MESSAGES FROM
GOD

What the Bible Reveals to You

AMERICAN BIBLE SOCIETY

Time Home Entertainment
PUBLISHER
Jim Childs
VICE PRESIDENT, BUSINESS DEVELOPMENT & STRATEGY
Steven Sandonato
EXECUTIVE DIRECTOR, MARKETING SERVICES
Carol Pittard
EXECUTIVE DIRECTOR, RETAIL & SPECIAL SALES
Tom Mifsud
EXECUTIVE PUBLISHING DIRECTOR
Joy Butts
EDITORIAL DIRECTOR
Stephen Koepp
EDITORIAL OPERATIONS DIRECTOR
Michael Q. Bullerdick
DIRECTOR, BOOKAZINE DEVELOPMENT & MARKETING
Laura Adam
FINANCE DIRECTOR
Glenn Buonocore
ASSOCIATE PUBLISHING DIRECTOR
Megan Pearlman
ASSISTANT GENERAL COUNSEL
Helen Wan
ASSISTANT DIRECTOR, SPECIAL SALES
Ilene Schreider
ASSOCIATE PRODUCTION MANAGER
Kimberly Marshall
DESIGN & PREPRESS MANAGER
Anne-Michelle Gallero
BRAND MANAGER
Nina Fleishman
ASSOCIATE PREPRESS MANAGER
Alex Voznesenskiy

General Editor
Christopher D. Hudson

Senior Editors
Kelly Knauer, Ben Irwin

Managing Editor
Carol Smith

Consulting Editors
Philip H. Towner, Ph.D.
Barbara Bernstengel, M.A.
Robert Hodgson, Ph.D.
Charles Houser, B.A.
Davina McDonald, M.A.
Thomas R. May, M.Div.
*With special thanks to the American Bible Committee
on Translation and Scholarship*

Contributing Writers
Stan Campbell
Stephen Clark
Robin Schmidt
Anita Palmer
Kimn Swenson-Golnick
Mia Littlejohn
Shannon Woodward
Carol Smith
Randy Southern

Design and Production
Mark Wainwright, Symbology Creative

special thanks: Katherine Barnet, Jeremy Biloon,
Susan Chodakiewicz, Rose Cirrincione, Lauren Hall Clark,
Jacqueline Fitzgerald, Christine Font, Jenna Goldberg,
Hillary Hirsch, Suzanne Janso, David Kahn, Mona Li,
Amy Mangus, Robert Marasco, Amy Migliaccio,
Nina Mistry, Dave Rozzelle, Ricardo Santiago,
Adriana Tierno, Vanessa Wu

© 2013 **Time Home Entertainment Inc.**
Published by Time Home Entertainment Inc.
135 West 50th Street • New York, NY 10020

Unless otherwise noted, all Scripture quotations are from the *Holy
Bible, Contemporary English Version* (CEV). Copyright 1995 by the
American Bible Society. Used by permission of the American Bible
Society. All rights reserved.

Scripture quotations marked NIV are taken from the *Holy Bible,
New International Version*, copyright © 1973, 1978, 1984 by the
International Bible Society.
Used by permission of Zondervan. All rights reserved.

ISBN 10: 1-60320-962-X   ISBN 13: 978-1-60320-962-5

We welcome your comments and suggestions about
Messages from God, please write to us at:
Messages from God
Attention: Book Editors
PO Box 11016
Des Moines, IA 50336-1016

If you would like to order any of our hardcover Collector's
Edition books, please call us at 1-800-327-6388 (Monday through
Friday, 7:00 a.m.– 8:00 p.m.; or Saturday, 7:00 a.m.– 6:00 p.m.
Central Time).

TABLE OF CONTENTS

INTRODUCTION

God has a message for you.

The Bible is a collection of books written by many different authors over a period of centuries. But these stories, poems, laws, and prophecies are not just a haphazard collection of literature. There is a deeper story—a thread holding all the pieces together. Behind each story is an important message from God that the authors wanted their readers to hear.

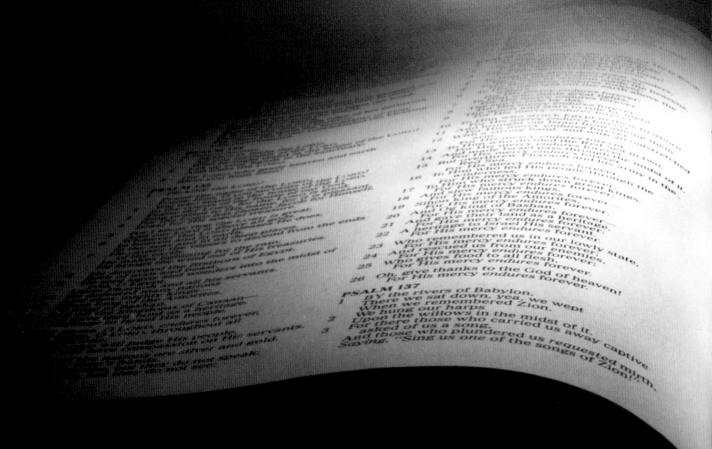

Yet because the Bible is an ancient book—and because of the cultural distance that separates us from those who wrote it—unearthing its deeper message is not always an easy task. Many of its stories may seem familiar to us, perhaps too familiar. We've heard them so many times that we don't stop long enough to ponder the hidden details or their implications. Other stories are both alarming and intriguing to us because they sound so foreign. How could God speak from a fiery bush? Why did he have one of his own prophets swallowed by a great fish? How can there be so much violence in the Bible? What purpose do angelic messengers serve? What was Jesus' real mission? And how could he have risen from the dead?

Messages from God takes you beyond the "what" of Scripture's most iconic stories and delves into the "why." From the first moments of creation to Israel's exodus from Egypt, from the Old Testament warriors to the "Prince of Peace" himself, you'll decode and discover the deeper meaning of each story and see how it fits into the larger storyline of Scripture.

Whatever else the Bible may be, it is at its core a story of rescue and salvation. It's about God's relationship with the world he made—a world that went tragically wrong when sin entered the world and ruptured humankind's relationship with God. It's about God's promise to rescue people and renew the world—a promise that, according to the Bible, was fulfilled in the life, death, and resurrection of Jesus. Every story plays into this larger story line in its own way, reinforcing the overarching message of the Bible—that God wants us to be reconciled to him and to have our relationship with him restored.

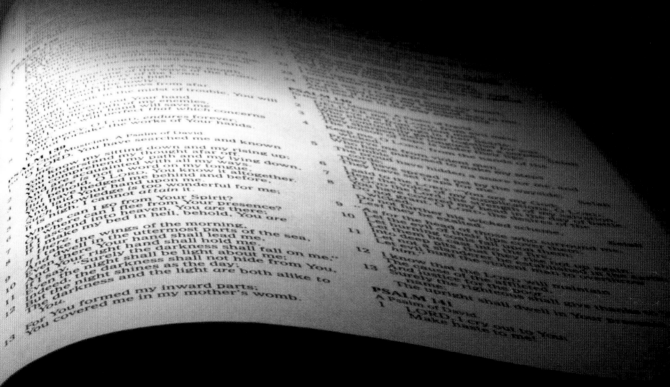

"Would it not be strange
if a universe without
purpose accidentally
created humans who are
so obsessed with purpose?"

Sir John Templeton,
*The Humble Approach: Scientists
Discover God*

the wonders of

CREA

"In the beginning God." These four words launch us into the
sweeping story of the Bible. The first chapter in the book of Genesis
describes God creating the world in six days. Many scholars think
the Genesis story is not so much about the *how* of creation as it is
about the *why* and, more importantly, the *who*.

CH 1

TION

As told in Genesis 1, God moves with purpose. He spends three days forming the world—separating day from night, water below from water above, land from sea—and three days filling it with every creature imaginable. Day six reveals a deeper meaning behind God's creative activity: making the world so he can share it with human beings. Men and women are created to be like himself, to rule and care for the earth on God's behalf.

The Bible presents the universe in all its splendor, our world and all its wonders, our human bodies and all their complicated parts, this vast yet intricate creation—all springing from an intelligent being operating with a deliberate design and purpose. Creation, we are told, is the work of the mind and hand of God.

GOD'S
creation

A message from
THE BIBLE

ISAIAH 66:1–2a
The Lord said:
Heaven is my throne;
   the earth is my footstool.
What kind of house
could you build for me?
   In what place will I rest?
I have made everything;
that's how it all came to be.
   I, the Lord, have spoken.

"A common-sense and satisfying interpretation of our world suggests the designing hand of a super intelligence."

— Owen Gingerich, senior emeritus astronomer at the Smithsonian Astrophysical Observatory, "Dare a Scientist Believe in Design?" in *Evidence of Purpose*

"I do not believe that any scientists who examined the evidence would fail to draw the inference that the laws of nuclear physics have been deliberately designed with regard to the consequences they produce inside stars."

— Sir Fred Hoyle, *Annual Review of Astronomy and Astrophysics*

"A universe aiming at the production of man implies a mind directing it. Though man is not at the physical center of the universe, he appears to be at the center of its purpose."

— Robert M. Augros and George N. Stanciu, *The New Story of Science*

"It is hard to resist the impression that the present structure of the universe, apparently so sensitive to minor alterations in numbers, has been rather carefully thought out . . . The seemingly miraculous concurrence of these numerical values must remain the most compelling evidence for cosmic design."

— Paul Davies, *The Cosmic Blueprint: New Discoveries in Nature's Creative Ability to Order the Universe*

ISAIAH 45:18
The Lord alone is God!
He created the heavens
and made a world
where people can live,
instead of creating
an empty desert.
The Lord alone is God;
there are no others.

WHAT'S THE POINT?

Scientists study how and when the world came into being. Scripture wants to show us who's behind it all. According to the Bible, we are not here by accident. Some scholars think Genesis 1 depicts the world as God's cosmic temple, where he comes to rest on the seventh day and dwell with human beings. This idea sets the tone for the rest of the biblical story. After things go wrong in Genesis 3, God sets out to restore the world so he can dwell with us again (Revelation 21:3).

Source: *The Case for a Creator* written by Lee Strobel (2004, Zondervan).

THE MOON

AND THE SUN

(AND THE GOD WHO RULES THEM BOTH)

The writer of Genesis 1 wasn't afraid to challenge the conventional wisdom of his day. For example, many in the ancient world worshiped the moon and sun as divine beings. Yet the Bible mentions both in its creation account. (They're the *"two powerful lights"* in Genesis 1:16.) This may be Scripture's way of challenging their divinity by indicating that they are just created objects and that there is only one true God.

THE MOON

The moon plays a mystifying role in our lives on earth. It regulates our seasons by stabilizing the tilt of the earth's axis. Imagine our world without it: instead of a one-and-a-half-degree tilt, the earth might swing like an off-kilter pendulum, its temperature and climate as erratic as its trajectory. The moon also plays an important role in controlling the tides. Without it, our oceans could surge and slosh like bathtub water at the mercy of a playful child. In short, the moon keeps the earth habitable for us.

Some ancient civilizations regarded the moon as divine. The Sumerians, one of the earliest civilizations, identified the moon with the god Nanna. Nanna's seat of worship was Ur (a city in modern-day Iraq identified today as Tell el Muqayyar). According to Genesis 11:31, Ur was also the home of Israel's founding patriarch, Abraham.

THE SUN

Earth's sun is a star—the star closest to us and thus the brightest star that we see. In fact, it makes up 98 percent of the mass of our solar system (more than one million earths could fit in the sun). Of all the mysteries built into the delicate mechanism of our universe, one of the greatest is the precision of the distance between the earth and the sun—it is perfectly balanced to support human life. Closer, and it would be impossible to keep water on our planet from evaporating or even boiling away. Farther, and earth's water would freeze solid.

It was common practice in the ancient Near Eastern world to deify forces of nature. Many of Israel's neighbors—the Accadians, Assyrians, and Babylonians (all of whom are mentioned in the Bible)—worshiped Shamash, the Mesopotamian sun god.

As Genesis 1 describes it, God made men and women on the sixth day of creation. He created humans to rule over the earth. But there is also another creation story in the Bible. Genesis 2 describes God forming the first man from *"some soil"* (and later the first woman from *"one of the man's ribs"*). It seems that human beings simultaneously stand out from the rest of creation and are intimately connected to it. But we were also made *"to be like [God] himself,"* according to Genesis 1:27, suggesting that human beings are uniquely precious to God. For people of faith, then, the miracle that is the human body stands as a testament to the Creator's care.

ONLY HUMAN?

"You are the one who put me together inside my mother's body."

Psalm 139:13

A message from
THE BIBLE

GENESIS 1:26–28

God said, "Now we will make humans, and they will be like us. We will let them rule the fish, the birds, and all other living creatures."

So God created humans to be like himself; he made men and women. God gave them his blessing and said: Have a lot of children! Fill the earth with people and bring it under your control. Rule over the fish in the ocean, the birds in the sky, and every animal on the earth.

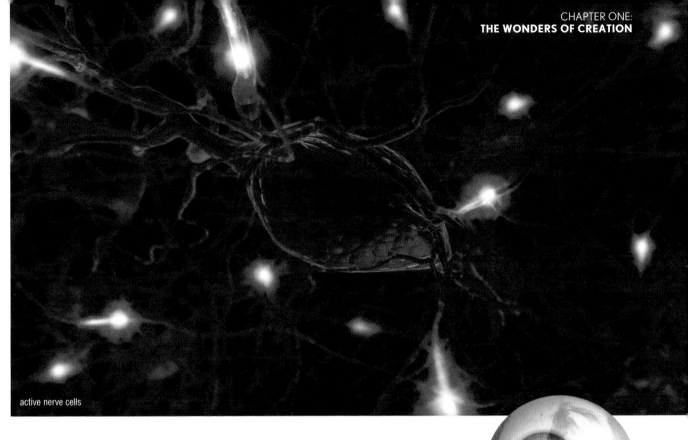

active nerve cells

OUR AMAZING BODIES

The adult human body is made up of 206 bones that provide its structure. Those bones are covered by twice as many muscles, without which the bones couldn't move. The body has systems to help us breathe, to circulate our blood, digest our food, and even heal ourselves when we are injured. We wear our largest organ of all on the outside—our skin. Most adults have at least 20 square feet of the stuff. It's waterproof, self-repairing, and it constantly renews and sheds itself.

IMAGE BEARERS

Some Bible translations use the phrase *"in God's image"* (Genesis 1:27) to describe the human race. In the ancient world, to bear a ruler's "image" (usually a royal coin or seal) was to be his authorized representative. To be made in God's image has significant implications for us; we are created to *"bring honor to him"* (Ephesians 1:12).

If you could harness the electrical output of your brain, it would power a 10-watt lightbulb. Your brain consumes 25 percent of all the oxygen used by your body.

Your body is 63 percent hydrogen and 25.5 percent oxygen. Also necessary are fluorine, silicon, tin, and vanadium.

If you start counting the twenty-seven trillion cells in your body, at the rate of ten per second, it will take you 100,000,000 years to finish.

The eye is essentially an opaque eyeball filled with a water-like fluid.

Your skin weighs 6 pounds and covers about 20 square feet.

You can sweat up to 3 gallons of perspiration per day.

One out of every 100 cells in your body works to defend you against disease. So if you weigh 150 pounds, 1½ pounds of you are for self-defense.

Fingerprints are built-in, easily accessible identity cards. They are a unique marker for a person, even for two otherwise identical twins.

JOB 10:11–12
Then you tied my bones together
with muscles
and covered them
with flesh and skin.
You, the source of my life,
showered me with kindness
and watched over me.

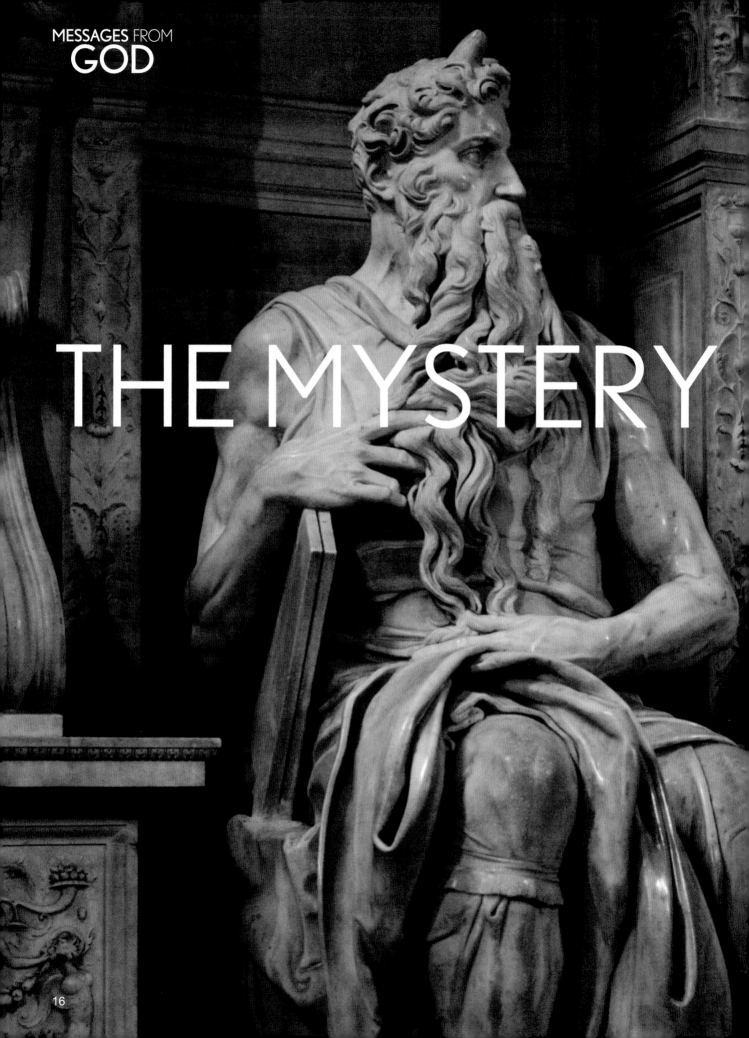

THE MYSTERY

OF MOSES

Moses the lawgiver looms large in the Old Testament, but he was an unlikely hero. According to the book of Exodus, Moses survived Pharaoh's (the King of Egypt) genocidal targeting of Hebrew boys— only to become a member of Pharaoh's household, cared for by Pharaoh's own daughter.

Years later, after having killed an Egyptian for beating a Hebrew slave, Moses fled to the wilderness to escape the wrath of Pharaoh. But there was someone even more powerful than Pharaoh waiting for Moses in the desert. There he met Israel's God, who enlisted Moses to rescue the Israelites from slavery in Egypt.

Moses' story sets the stage for everything that follows in the Bible. The Israelites' escape from Egypt, led by Moses, is the most dramatic act of deliverance in the Old Testament. God initiated and entered into a covenant with the Hebrews, forming them into a nation (Exodus 19:5), as demonstrated by the Ten Commandments chiseled in stone (Deuteronomy 5:1–22). The Ten Commandments define the relationship between God and the people and are the basis of the covenant.

For Christians, Moses prefigures another deliverer in the Bible: Jesus. Like Moses, Jesus is depicted as leading people out of the bondage of sin and God's condemnation and into a reconciled relationship with God. The New Testament suggests that Jesus is an even greater lawgiver than Moses.

But it all began with Moses, a timid shepherd hiding in the desert of Midian.

Statue of Moses, Michelangelo. Church of San Pietro in Vincoli in Rome, Italy.

THE **BURNING** BUSH

Just as the Bible is a book of marvels, it is a book of symbols. And surely among the most memorable of the great book's symbols is the incandescent moment when God first speaks to Moses in the form of a burning bush, summoning him to a life of service and faith.

Why did God choose to appear as a flame, a fire burning endlessly, without consuming the fuel that feeds its flames? After all, God could have chosen many avenues to speak to Moses: he could have appeared as a figure in a dream or a voice in a vision. He might have taken the form of a simple pilgrim on the road.

In this case, the medium itself is the message—at least part of it. Fire is a symbol of power and life. In the burning bush, Moses saw God's power over natural forces. But he also saw an unforgettable symbol of the endlessly replenishing power of faith.

VISION OF A PROMISED LAND

When God spoke to Moses in the burning bush, he reaffirmed that the ancient Israelites were his chosen people (Deuteronomy 7:8; 10:15) and offered Moses a vision of their future home, the land God had promised to their ancestors (Deuteronomy 8:1). *The LORD said: I will bring my people out of Egypt into a country where there is a lot of good land, rich with milk and honey. I will give them the land where the Canaanites, Hittites, Amorites, Perizzites, Hivites, and Jebusites now live. My people have begged for my help, and I have seen how cruel the Egyptians are to them. Now go to the king! I am sending you to lead my people out of his country* (Exodus 3:7a, 8b–10).

***Moses before the Pharaoh**, a 6th-century miniature from the *Syriac Bible* of Paris*

A message from
THE BIBLE

EXODUS 3:1–6

One day, Moses was taking care of the sheep and goats of his father-in-law Jethro, the priest of Midian, and Moses decided to lead them across the desert to Sinai, the holy mountain. There an angel of the LORD appeared to him from a burning bush. Moses saw that the bush was on fire, but it was not burning up. "This is strange!" he said to himself. "I'll go over and see why the bush isn't burning up."

When the LORD saw Moses coming near, he called him by name from the bush, and Moses answered, "Here I am."

God replied, "Don't come any closer. Take off your sandals—the ground where you are standing is holy. I am the God who was worshiped by your ancestors Abraham, Isaac, and Jacob."

Moses was afraid to look at God, and so he hid his face.

Statue of Moses and the Ten Commandments in Copenhagen at Our Lady's Church

MOSES' SHINING FACE

The people of Moses' day were afraid they would die if they stood in God's presence (Numbers 17:12–13). From Moses' experience, it was obvious that to encounter the divine was to be utterly transformed. When Moses came down from Mount Sinai after speaking with God, his face glowed so brightly that he had to cover it with a veil. He would remove the veil whenever he spoke with God and when he told the people what God had said (Exodus 34:33–35).

The New Testament draws a striking parallel between Jesus and Moses. One day, Jesus *"went up on a very high mountain"* where he was *"completely changed."* According to Matthew 17, Jesus' *"face was shining like the sun,"* much as Moses' face shone centuries before. A shining face was considered proof of an encounter with God.

WRITTEN IN STONE

Michelangelo was one of the great painters of the Renaissance. Yet his first love was not painting, but sculpture. While his pigments and frescoes might fade, he knew that marble would weather the ravages of time.

When John Keats sought an image for the enduring power of art, he found it not in a book or a painting but in a marble Grecian urn. "When old age shall this generation waste," he wrote, "Thou shalt remain."

When twentieth-century sculptor Gustav Borglum sought to create a monument to American presidents that would endure for the ages, he transformed an entire mountain—Mount Rushmore—into his canvas.

And when God wanted to convey the enduring power and value of the Ten Commandments that would guide his chosen people, he sought a meaningful way to signify his covenant relationship with them. His Commandments would not be written on papyrus, to decay and wither; they would be chiseled in stone. These Commandments were written to last, as meaningful for believers three thousand years in the future as they were for Moses, the man who first beheld them, and all the Israelites. The choice of stone communicated almost as much as the words that were etched upon it.

The significance of stone also figures into the story of Jesus, who is regarded by the New Testament authors as a lawgiver even greater than Moses (Hebrews 3:1–6).

Yet there is an even deeper meaning behind the medium chosen for the Ten Commandments. For though they were carved by the hand of God onto tablets of stone, the intended resting place of the Ten Commandments is that most evanescent, if eternal, of locations: the human spirit. Centuries later, God, speaking to the people through the prophet Jeremiah, said: *"I will write my laws on their hearts and minds"* (Jeremiah 31:33b).

A message from
THE BIBLE
EXODUS 34:29–30
Moses came down from Mount Sinai, carrying the Ten Commandments. His face was shining brightly because the LORD had been speaking to him. . . . When Aaron and the others looked at Moses, they saw this, and they were afraid to go near him.

"The true work of art is but a shadow of the divine perfection."
~Michelangelo

THE ARK OF THE
COVENANT

The ark of the covenant was, in the simplest terms, a piece of furniture, an ornate chest placed in the innermost chamber of the tabernacle, or sacred tent, the portable temple used by the Hebrews as they wandered in the desert on their journey to the land of Canaan. The ark was crafted to house the stone tablets of the Ten Commandments; later it was placed in a special chamber in Solomon's Temple in Jerusalem.

The innermost chambers of both the traveling tabernacle and Solomon's Temple were full of religious significance. They were seen by the ancient Israelites as the exact place where God actually lived among them (Exodus 25:22; Numbers 7:89).

CAN'T TOUCH THIS!

Like Mount Sinai, which the people could not set foot on or touch when God was present, the ark was considered untouchable. In fact, there were extensive instructions given about how to carry the ark as the people traveled: they were to use special poles that slid through loops attached to the ark, and it was to be borne only by Levitical priests (Deuteronomy 10:8; 1 Chronicles 15:2).

The Bible records several instances in which people failed to honor the no-touch zone. The Philistines, longtime enemies of the Israelites, once captured the ark—only to find the cities where they stashed it had suffered wild afflictions; some of the people died just looking inside the sacred chest.

In fact, the Philistines passed the ark around like a hot potato until they finally, desperately, sent it back to the Israelites (1 Samuel 5–7). During the reign of King David, an attempt was made to transport the ark to Jerusalem on a cart, rather than by the poles designed to carry it. When the cart hit a bump, one of the men assigned by David to guide the cart reached out to steady it—and was immediately struck dead (1 Chronicles 13).

While the movie *Raiders of the Lost Ark* portrayed the power inherent in the ancient ark of the covenant, it also indicated that the sacred chest is now stored in some obscure and forgotten corner of a US government warehouse. Since this is a fictional story, there's no evidence, as far as we know, to support that the original ark still exists.

THE POWER OF THE ARK

The materials used to make the ark of the covenant (Exodus 25:10–22) offer insight into its true significance. The ark was built from acacia wood and gold—the same materials as the sacred tent (or tabernacle) where God was said to live among his people.

Years later, King Hezekiah of Judah connected the ark of the covenant to God's throne: *"Lᴏʀᴅ God of Israel, your throne is above the winged creatures [on the chest's cover]"* (2 Kings 19:15). In other words, the Israelites believed that when the ark of the covenant was near, they were as close as they could get to the presence of God.

While the long-lost ark offers endless fascination for adventurers, treasure hunters, and archaeologists alike, the writers of the New Testament were less concerned by its disappearance. The author of Hebrews depicts Jesus entering the most holy place of a *"much better tent"* on behalf of the entire human race (Hebrews 9:11–12). Thus for Christians, the ark of the covenant is no longer needed as a reminder of God's presence; Jesus himself became the presence of God among his people (John 1:14).

MANY FORMS
ONE VOICE

The Infant Samuel Being Offered to the High Priest Eli
Gothic manuscript, 15th century
Bibliothèque Nationale, Paris, France

The God who addressed Moses from a burning bush appears and communicates through many other forms as the biblical story progresses. These appearances often reveal important aspects of God's character.

The fiery bush was a sign of God's holiness. The Ten Commandments, chiseled into stone, suggested the enduring power of God's spoken word—and any covenant he made with the people (see page 21).

Perhaps there was a touch of humor in God's treatment of the prophet Balaam, to whom he spoke through a donkey with a warning to tell the King of Moab what God wanted him to say (Numbers 22).

On other occasions, God spoke simply and directly, as he did with a boy named Samuel (see 1 Samuel 3). Perhaps this was a sign of Samuel's significance, for this great leader served as a bridge between two important eras in the history of the Israelites. Samuel was the last judge of Israel, and he would one day anoint Israel's first king.

Samuel's close encounter with God began when he was a child serving in the tabernacle. It was there that God first spoke to him, calling his name in the night. The Bible notes that such dreams and visions were rare at that time in Israel's history. God, it seemed, no longer spoke to his people. Meanwhile, the Israelites' enemies, the Philistines, kept them in subjugation.

So when Samuel heard someone calling his name in the darkness, he ran to his guardian, the old priest Eli, to see what he needed. But the old man sent him back to bed.

Three times this happened. Finally, Eli told Samuel to answer the voice and listen carefully. Samuel did and, for the first time in years, the voice of God was heard in the land of Israel.

The message Samuel received was stern: Eli and his corrupt sons, Hophni and Phinehas, had failed in their priestly duties. As a result, woe would be visited upon the land. And so it was that the Israelites rose in rebellion against the Philistines, only to lose two mighty battles. But they lost something far more precious than a battle: the Philistines seized the ark of the covenant, the most sacred vessel of the Hebrews.

When the old priest Eli heard the news, he fell from his chair, broke his neck, and died. His sons were struck down for their wickedness. But God raised up Samuel—who had heard his voice and heeded his call—and made him the foremost leader of Israel. In time, Samuel would lead the Israelites to victory over the Philistines.

Thus from Moses to Samuel—and beyond—God appeared and communicated through different forms. But these appearances all have one thing in common: each marks a decisive turning point in the biblical story.

A message from
THE BIBLE
1 SAMUEL 3:1–11

Samuel served the LORD by helping Eli the priest, who was by that time almost blind. In those days, the LORD hardly ever spoke directly to people, and he did not appear to them in dreams very often. But one night, Eli was asleep in his room, and Samuel was sleeping on a mat near the sacred chest in the LORD's house. They had not been asleep very long when the LORD called out Samuel's name. "Here I am!" Samuel answered. Then he ran to Eli and said, "Here I am. What do you want?"

"I didn't call you," Eli answered. "Go back to bed.". . .

The LORD had not spoken to Samuel before, and Samuel did not recognize the voice . . .

Eli finally realized that it was the LORD who was speaking to Samuel. So he said, "Go back and lie down! If someone speaks to you again, answer, 'I'm listening, LORD. What do you want me to do?'"

Once again Samuel went back and lay down.

The LORD then stood beside Samuel and called out as he had done before, "Samuel! Samuel!"

"I'm listening," Samuel answered. "What do you want me to do?"

The LORD said: "Samuel, I am going to do something in Israel that will shock everyone who hears about it!"

PARTING
THE WATERS
(crossing the Red Sea)

The early part of the twenty-first century offers chilling testimony to the devastating power of water. A tsunami in the Indian Ocean killed more than 225,000 people in 2004. Nine months later, Hurricane Katrina submerged one of America's historic cities. Another tsunami struck in 2011, killing thousands and causing a nuclear meltdown at a power plant in Japan.

These are powers that dwarf those of humankind, reducing our works to child's play. In the face of a hurricane's raging winds, our strongest levees, dams, and canals offer little protection.

Yet the Bible describes a power greater than that of tsunamis and hurricanes. Some of the most memorable stories in the Old Testament describe nature's law being suspended as the forces of mass, gravity, and inertia are bent in submission to the commands of God and his prophets.

MOSES PARTS THE RED SEA

After the plagues devastated Egypt, Pharaoh not only allowed the Israelites to leave, he demanded that they do so. But his royal anger quickly subsided and, realizing that he was losing his slave population, Pharaoh sent his army to retrieve them.

With the entire Egyptian army on their heels and the Red Sea spread out before them, the Israelites were trapped, and panic quickly spread. At God's command, Moses held his staff over the waters and the sea parted, rising in two towering liquid walls with a path of dry ground between them. The Israelites quickly passed through, while the army that followed was swallowed up as the waters returned to their natural state. (Read Exodus 14.)

Though numerous theories have been offered to explain how the waters could have been parted, the crossing of the Red Sea defies easy understanding. Still, there is a deeper meaning behind the remarkable events of Exodus 14.

For many in the ancient world, the sea was synonymous with the abyss. Chaos resided in its watery depths; it was regarded with fear and misgiving. The exodus story served as a reminder to future generations of Israelites that the God who led their ancestors out of Egypt was also the God of the abyss; the sea was no match for him. God led his people through its depths—through the chaos—and into freedom.

But there is another important element of the story. After the last Israelite had crossed over, God told Moses to stretch his arm over the sea once more, sending a wall of water crashing down on the Egyptian pursuers. Not only did this decimate Pharaoh's army; it closed off the Israelites' route of return to the only home they had known for more than 400 years. Now, camped on the other side of the sea, there was no turning back.

A message from
THE BIBLE

EXODUS 14:19-22

All this time God's angel had gone ahead of Israel's army, but now he moved behind them. A large cloud had also gone ahead of them, but now it moved between the Egyptians and the Israelites. The cloud gave light to the Israelites, but made it dark for the Egyptians, and during the night they could not come any closer.

Moses stretched his arm over the sea, and the LORD sent a strong east wind that blew all night until there was dry land where the water had been. The sea opened up, and the Israelites walked through on dry land with a wall of water on each side.

EXODUS 14:30

On that day, when the Israelites saw the bodies of the Egyptians washed up on the shore, they knew that the LORD had saved them.

above: *The Crossing of the Red Sea*, 1634
Nicolas Poussin

27

DECODING

CH **3**

ANCIENT STORIES

In the early years of the eleventh century, England's King Canute grew weary of the flattery of fawning courtiers. When they dared tell him that even the sea would obey his commands, he decided that actions speak louder than words: the king had his servants carry his royal chair to the seaside as the tide rolled in.

There sat Canute, ordering the waves to stop. Yet in rolled the breakers, crashing against the shore until small waves were licking at his feet. Canute's attendants were forced into an embarrassing silence. The monarch had made his point: he was powerless to control the forces of nature.

Again and again, the Bible describes God as not only engaged in the affairs of this world but also able to orchestrate them in astonishing ways—even defying the laws of nature. At God's command, floodwaters covered the earth. An elderly couple gave birth to a miracle baby. A great fish swallowed a runaway prophet—who lived to tell about it.

Some of these phenomenal accounts are filled with joy, others with sober judgment. Behind each lies a deeper meaning for discerning readers to discover.

The Destruction of Sodom by Fire
Musee des Beaux-Arts, Orleans, France

ET VOLVCRM / DI SE ET IIM / ID SE CA

CRESSVS E NOE SEM CH ARE

NOAH'S ARK

Noah's ark—the vast vessel that floats at the center of a story shared by Jews, Christians, and Muslims—is one of the most familiar images in the world. It features prominently in children's storybooks, often depicted as a round-bellied boat bobbing on the sea, with knobby-headed giraffes and plush lions peering from its windows, all framed by a cheery rainbow. But the real story is much darker. Dismayed by how evil humans had become, God vowed to destroy every last person with a catastrophic flood—except for one family.

CREATION REBOOTED

The flood is as much a story of preservation and rescue as it is one of judgment and destruction. Noah and his family, along with a remnant of every kind of animal, were preserved—spared from God's judgment. This signals more than just the fact that Noah was a good person. (He was, according to Genesis 6:9, *"the only person who lived right and obeyed God."*) It was also an indication that God wasn't ready to give up on his creation. He intended to make a new start with Noah.

Some scholars see a parallel between Noah and Adam. After the flood, God gave Noah the same command he had given Adam at the beginning of creation: *"Have a lot of children and grandchildren, so people will live everywhere on this earth"* (Genesis 9:1).

STRANGE PARALLELS

Many ancient cultures told stories of a great primeval flood. One well-known example is the Sumerian *Epic of Gilgamesh*, written sometime between 1300 BC and 1000 BC. Yet the biblical flood story is unique in its focus on Noah and his ark—and, by implication, God's determination to save a remnant of humanity.

The flood story has other interesting parallels within the Bible itself. In Exodus 2, for example, Moses' mother put him in a basket on the edge of the Nile River, hoping to spare him from Pharaoh's murderous campaign. The Hebrew word used to describe Moses' basket is the same used for Noah's ark. Some scholars think the writer of Exodus presented Moses as a second Noah, marking yet another decisive moment in the biblical story.

RAINBOW

One of the most iconic images from the story of Noah's ark is the rainbow that appeared after the flood as a sign of God's promise never again to destroy the earth with a flood (Genesis 9:12–17). According to the writer of Genesis, the rainbow was a reminder not just to Noah and his descendants but also to God: *"When I see the rainbow in the sky, I will always remember the promise that I have made to every living creature"* (9:16).

Interestingly, the Hebrew word for "rainbow" is also the word for a warrior's bow. Some scholars have suggested that by flooding the earth, God in effect declared war on his creation. Once the judgment was completed, however, God hung this particular weapon in the sky, a reminder to all that it will not be taken down again.

Mount Ararat? Where's That At?

A volcano and one of the tallest mountains in the Middle East, modern-day Mount Ararat, in Eastern Turkey, is the most popular site for modern ark hunters. It's so mammoth, it has a permanent ice cap, which could conceal an ancient artifact like the ark.

On the other hand, some scholars believe the Bible may have been referring not to Mount Ararat but rather to Urartu, an ancient kingdom in this mountainous region.

Durupinar, a canoe-shaped formation named for the Turkish captain who discovered it eighteen miles south of Greater Ararat, is also a possible site.

Another theory focuses on Al Judi, also known as Mount Cudi, a peak in southeastern Turkey. Some ark hunters have even considered Ethiopia and Ireland as possible locations for the legendary ark.

Birds Entering the Ark, Mosaic, Venice, Italy

MIRACLE BABIES
of the Bible

Impossible pregnancies have a way of cropping up again and again in the Bible. Perhaps the best-known story is that of Sarah and her husband, Abraham, who were quite old when God promised them a child of their own. Their miracle baby would leave a legacy of countless descendants, a whole nation.

Despite the natural odds, God's promise came to pass. At the age of ninety, Sarah gave birth to Isaac.

It's not hard to imagine how much difficulty Sarah and Abraham had believing it would happen. At times they laughed at the idea. On other occasions, they schemed of ways to "help" the promise along.

But it was not Abraham and Sarah's scheming that brought about the promised pregnancy. One of the important messages of their story is that God is always faithful, even when his people are not.

Abraham first received the promise of a child directly from God. Later, he played host to guests who confirmed Sarah's impending pregnancy. According to Genesis 18, three men appeared at the home of Abraham and Sarah. One of those men was identified as *"the Lord"*; the other two were presumed to be angels. It was during this encounter that Sarah overheard the conversation and laughed to herself—only to be heard by their guests and confronted about her willingness to trust in God.

Why do miraculous pregnancies recur throughout the Bible? Perhaps they serve to remind us of God's special concern for the vulnerable. In the ancient Near East, failure to produce a child was considered a terrible tragedy, especially for women for whom barrenness was a sign of disgrace. Infertility threatened the preservation of the family name. God, however, brought honor to the following women:

REBEKAH After having difficulty conceiving (Genesis 25:21), Rebekah and her husband, Isaac (Abraham and Sarah's son), gave birth to twin boys: Jacob, one of the patriarchs of Israel, and Esau.

WIFE OF MANOAH AND MOTHER OF SAMSON She was not able to have children, but *"an angel from the Lord appeared to her"* and told her that she would give birth to a son who would belong to God (Judges 13:3).

HANNAH Her years of infertility ended with the promise spoken by a priest named Eli (1 Samuel 1:17). Shortly afterward, Hannah conceived and bore a son, Samuel, whose name means "God heard." Samuel became a great prophet and anointed two kings of Israel. Hannah's prayer to God after the birth of her son highlights one deeper purpose for such impossible pregnancies: God will *"lift the poor . . . and give them places of honor"* (1 Samuel 2:8).

MARY In the New Testament, an angel appeared to Mary, a young virgin in Nazareth, who was betrothed to Joseph. She was told that she would have a son who would be called Jesus and who would be the holy Son of God. The Holy Spirit would come down and God's power would overcome her. Like Hannah, Mary proclaims that God *"puts humble people in places of power"* (Luke 1:52).

ELIZABETH Mary's cousin Elizabeth conceived after God spoke to her husband in the temple. Both Zechariah and Elizabeth were quite old when they gave birth to their son—who grew up to be John the Baptist (Luke 1:5–25, 57–80).

The Three Angels Appearing to Abraham, Giambattista Tiepolo (1696–1770)

SODOM and GOMORRAH

The Destruction of Sodom and Gomorrah, John Martin, 1852

Located along the salty flats near the Dead Sea, the two cities of Sodom and Gomorrah were notorious in biblical times for the extravagant misdeeds of their inhabitants. Today, the cities' names are synonymous with iniquity. But what was the true story behind their destruction?

According to the Bible, Abraham, the great ancestor of the Israelites and other Semitic tribes, was disturbed when he learned that God intended to destroy Sodom and Gomorrah, where his nephew Lot lived. Abraham negotiated with God, asking him to spare the cities if ten righteous people could be found living in them. God agreed, but the census of the righteous did not even reach two digits. Lot, having been warned, fled with his wife and two unmarried daughters. His wife looked back and was destroyed; only Lot and his daughters escaped death (Genesis 19).

A PROPHET'S CLUE

Centuries later, the prophet Ezekiel addressed the people of Jerusalem, comparing their evil to that of Sodom (see Ezekiel 16). In his diatribe, he revealed the true nature of Sodom's sin, which prompted God to decimate the city with burning sulfur:

"They were arrogant and spoiled; they had everything they needed and still refused to help the poor and needy. They thought they were better than everyone else, and they did things I hate. And so I destroyed them" (Ezekiel 16:49–50).

Alarmingly for his audience, Ezekiel declared that Sodom's sin was nothing compared to Jerusalem's unfaithfulness: *"Your evil ways have made both Sodom and Samaria look innocent"* (16:51). But Ezekiel's message held out a glimmer of hope for Sodom, which meant there was hope for Jerusalem, too: *"Someday I will bless Sodom and Samaria and their nearby villages. I will also bless you, Jerusalem"* (16:53).

A message from
THE BIBLE

GENESIS 19:27–29

That same morning Abraham got up and went to the place where he had stood and spoken with the LORD. He looked down toward Sodom and Gomorrah and saw smoke rising from all over the land—it was like a flaming furnace.

When God destroyed the cities of the valley where Lot lived, he remembered his promise to Abraham and saved Lot from the terrible destruction.

The Dead Sea, Israel

REMNANTS FOUND?

In the 1960s and 1970s, archaeologist Paul W. Lapp discovered what he believed to be the location of the destroyed cities. The area south of the Dead Sea contains asphalt, sulfur (brimstone), petroleum, tar pits, and natural gas.

THE PROPHET ELIJAH

Elijah is one of the most renowned prophets in the Old Testament. He is famous not just for standing up to the wicked King Ahab and his wife Jezebel, but for the many astonishing miracles attributed to him.

So great was Elijah's influence that his name is invoked dozens of times in the New Testament. Both Jesus and his forerunner John the Baptist were subjects of speculation that Elijah had returned—an understandable assumption, since the Old Testament describes Elijah being taken up to heaven without ever dying (2 Kings 2:1–18). Indeed, Elijah's remarkable life drew parallels to those who came before and after him.

- Like Moses, Elijah was forced to flee to the desert to escape an angry ruler—in Elijah's case, Queen Jezebel. Both men had an encounter with God in the desert, but Elijah's was very different. This time, instead of speaking from a burning bush, God came in the form of a gentle breeze. (Read 1 Kings 19:1–18).

- During a severe drought, Elijah asked a starving Phoenician woman to feed him, promising that her meager stores would not run out before the rain returned (1 Kings 17:8–16). What is remarkable about this story is not just the miraculous multiplication of the woman's food but also the fact that Elijah made such a gesture toward a non-Jewish woman. Years later, Jesus used this very story to justify his association with Gentiles (see Luke 4:23–27).

- When Elijah needed to cross the Jordan, he parted the waters, recalling Moses' miraculous parting of the Red Sea. (Read 2 Kings 2:1–8.)

- Elijah's prayers restored life to a dead boy—making Elijah one of only two people in the Old Testament said to have raised the dead. (The other was Elisha.) Rumors of such miracles would not be whispered again until the time of Jesus. (Read 1 Kings 17:17–24.)

Elijah was a bearer of God's message to the Israelites. Though they had strayed from their allegiance to God and were worshiping idols—in particular the false god Baal—God wanted them back. Elijah had been entrusted with the task of calling these rebellious, but deeply loved, people back to their faith in God.

On God's behalf, Elijah challenged the prophets of Baal to a confrontation. Each would prepare a sacrifice and pray that his god would supply the fire to burn up those sacrifices. So confident was Elijah that he drenched his altar with water. While the opposing altar remained cold, God demonstrated his power by burning not only the wood but the sacrifice and the altar as well. (Read 1 Kings 18:3–40.)

Elijah's was a life like no other. So too was his exit. Rather than die, he was carried to heaven in a chariot. It was this wondrous ascent into heaven that inspired the moving spiritual, "Swing Low, Sweet Chariot." (Read 2 Kings 2:1–18.)

JONAH
in the FISH

Jonah's futile flight from God resulted in his being swallowed by a large fish. It is one of the better-known stories of the Old Testament. Jonah hesitated to follow God's direction, mainly because God had called him to preach to the residents of Nineveh, capital of Israel's enemy, Assyria.

But there is a surprising twist to the story—often overlooked in its retelling—that shines a surprising light on its deeper meaning.

Depiction of Jonah
Nicholas of Verdun
Verdun Altar, Klosterneuberg Abbey, Austria

A message from
THE BIBLE
JONAH 1:1–5, 12—2:10

One day the LORD told Jonah, the son of Amittai, to go to the great city of Nineveh and say to the people, "The LORD has seen your terrible sins. You are doomed!"

Instead, Jonah ran from the LORD. He went to the seaport of Joppa and found a ship that was going to Spain. So he paid his fare, then got on the ship and sailed away to escape.

But the LORD made a strong wind blow, and such a bad storm came up that the ship was about to be broken to pieces. The sailors were frightened, and they all started praying to their gods. They even threw the ship's cargo overboard to make the ship lighter. . . . Jonah told them, "Throw me into the sea, and it will calm down. I'm the cause of this terrible storm."

The sailors tried their best to row to the shore. But they could not do it, and the storm kept getting worse every minute. So they prayed to the LORD, "Please don't let us drown for taking this man's life. Don't hold us guilty for killing an innocent man. All of this happened because you wanted it to." Then they threw Jonah overboard, and the sea calmed down. The sailors were so terrified that they offered a sacrifice to the LORD and made all kinds of promises.

The LORD sent a big fish to swallow Jonah, and Jonah was inside the fish for three days and three nights.

From inside the fish, Jonah prayed to the LORD his God:

When I was in trouble, LORD, I prayed to you, and you listened to me. From deep in the world of the dead, I begged for your help, and you answered my prayer. You threw me down to the bottom of the sea. The water was churning all around; I was completely covered by your mighty waves. I thought I was swept away from your sight, never again to see your holy temple. I was almost drowned by the swirling waters that surrounded me. Seaweed had wrapped around my head. I had sunk down deep below the mountains beneath the sea. I knew that forever, I would be a prisoner there. But, you, LORD God, rescued me from that pit. When my life was slipping away, I remembered you—and in your holy temple you heard my prayer. All who worship worthless idols turn from the God who offers them mercy. But with shouts of praise, I will offer a sacrifice to you, my LORD. I will keep my promise, because you are the one with power to save.

The LORD commanded the fish to vomit up Jonah on the shore. And it did.

Jonah is best known to most people for his sojourn in the belly of a great fish. Remarkably, Jonah is said to have survived three days before the fish regurgitated him onto a beach—alive. After his temporary experience as fish food, Jonah went on to do what God had called him to do: he went to Nineveh and preached a *"message of doom"* (Jonah 3:2).

But here the story takes an unexpected turn: the people of Nineveh listened to Jonah. They repented—even the king. As a result, God took pity on Nineveh and spared the city.

Jonah was aghast. It was Nineveh, after all! If anyone deserved to be annihilated, surely it was the Assyrians! In the final scene, Jonah revealed why he didn't want to go to Nineveh in the first place—not because he was afraid of the Assyrians, but because he was afraid God would have mercy on them.

Jonah's story is a cautionary tale against bigotry. It served as a warning to the people of Israel not to assume they were the only ones God cared about. As Jonah observed (bitterly, in his case), *"You are a kind and merciful God, and you are very patient. You always show love, and you don't like to punish anyone"* (4:2).

Years later, a similar choice had to be made when the first Christians were given an opportunity to take the message of Jesus to Gentiles. Unlike Jonah, however, they willingly rose to the occasion (see Acts 10 and 13:42–48).

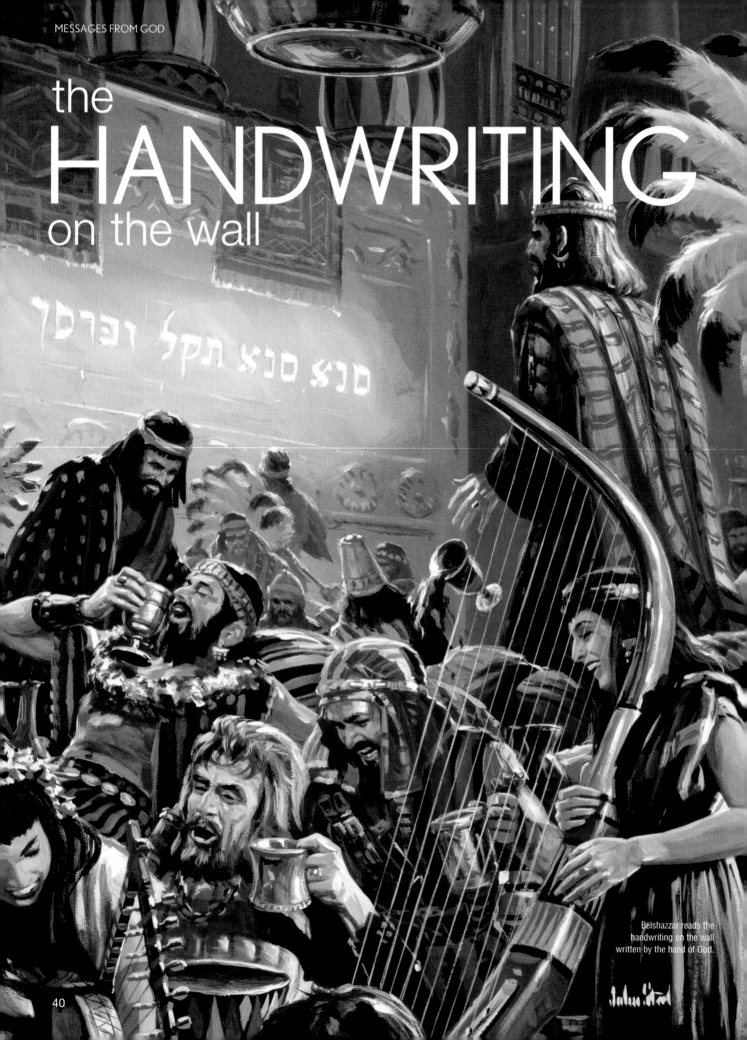

the HANDWRITING
on the wall

מנא מנא תקל ופרסין

Belshazzar reads the
handwriting on the wall
written by the hand of God.

Taken captive by the Babylonians when they conquered Jerusalem, Daniel became a chief advisor, prophet, and interpreter of dreams. Through the cunning of his rivals, he was cast into a den of lions, and three of his colleagues were thrown into a fiery furnace—ordeals they survived through God's grace.

After Jerusalem's fall (586 BC), God's voice was rarely heard in the Old Testament. Indeed, as far as we know, God never spoke directly to Daniel. But his story was meant to remind readers that God hadn't abandoned his people. Thus while God's voice could not be heard audibly, Daniel served as a translator through whom a terrible message and a terrible fate were visited upon those who mocked the Lord.

Daniel was an Israelite, born in Jerusalem to one of the noble families of the kingdom of Judah. In those times, the days of the Babylonian Captivity, the Israelites were subservient to the Assyrians under King Nebuchadnezzar. Daniel and three other noble youths, along with other young men from leading Jewish families, were taken to Babylon, Nebuchadnezzar's capital, as hostages. There they were trained in the pagan arts by the magi, the astrologer-priests—yet they remained loyal to the God of Israel.

Daniel rose high in the councils of Babylon, and he demonstrated a gift for interpreting dreams and visions. So it was natural that when God spoke to the court of Nebuchadnezzar's son, King Belshazzar, in a most mysterious way, Daniel would be called in to translate.

The story of Belshazzar's feast is one of the great scenes of the Bible: with the army of Cyrus the Persian threatening the city, Belshazzar and a host of his nobles and their concubines descended into debauchery, reveling in an enormous, drunken feast.

At the height of the party, Belshazzar called for the sacred vessels of the Israelites, stolen when Solomon's Temple in Jerusalem was sacked. He and his cohorts drank wine from them, even as they sang the praises of their pagan gods and roared over the fate of the fallen Hebrews.

Yet every tongue fell silent when, out of nowhere, a hand appeared and wrote four words on the wall of the chamber: *Mene, mene, tekel, parsin*. Then, as quickly as it had appeared, the mysterious hand vanished.

No one could make sense of the words. Finally, Daniel was summoned. The words, he told Belshazzar, were severe indeed. His kingdom would be divided; his rule would come to an end. That very night Belshazzar was slain, and the Persians conquered Babylon.

In the ancient world, it was widely assumed that when you conquered another nation, you conquered their gods as well. Belshazzar foolishly thought he could desecrate the Israelites' sacred vessels because their god had abandoned them—or was too impotent to intervene. Belshazzar's untimely demise was a sober reminder that Israel's God was by no means out of the picture.

A message from
THE BIBLE

DANIEL 5:22–24

King Belshazzar, you knew all of this, but you still refused to honor the Lord who rules from heaven. Instead, you turned against him and ordered the cups from his temple to be brought here, so that you and your wives and officials could drink wine from them. You praised idols made of silver, gold, bronze, iron, wood, and stone, even though they cannot see or hear or think. You refused to worship the God who gives you breath and controls everything you do. That's why he sent the hand to write this message on the wall.

Persian and Median warriors. Relief from the Audience Hall of Darius I (Apadana), eastern stairway. Achaemenid dynasty, 6th–5th c. BC. Persepolis, Iran

SECRET REASONS

FOR WAR

"I hate war as only a soldier who has lived it can, as one who has seen its brutality, its futility, its stupidity." General Dwight D. Eisenhower spoke these words shortly after the end of World War II. Those who have fought in war know better than anyone what a horrific experience it is. That's why many readers are shocked by all the violence they find in the Bible.

Generally, Scripture takes a dim view of warfare. Human violence is said to be one of the main reasons God decided to flood the world and start over (Genesis 6:11–13). In the New Testament, Jesus rebuked Peter for picking up a sword. *"Anyone who lives by fighting will die by fighting,"* he warned (Matthew 26:52).

Yet Israel's path to the Promised Land was marked by violent conflict. What deeper meaning lies behind these famous tales of war? How do the Bible's greatest military heroes—men like Joshua, Samson, and David—fit into the larger story?

the battles of
JOSHUA

No other leader of the Israelites created more unexpected or grandiose battle strategies than Joshua, the man God chose to be Moses' successor. Even when we first meet Joshua, he is in the midst of battle, soon after the Amalekites attacked the Israelites at Rephidim (see Exodus 17:8–16). Joshua was first and foremost a soldier. He led the Israelites as they fought to secure their claim to the land God had promised them.

Some experts think Joshua's bloody campaign should be read in light of passages such as Leviticus 18, where Moses listed a series of "disgusting practices" that the Canaanites (the land's occupants) followed, thus necessitating their eviction. As pagans, the Canaanites were regarded as a dangerous influence; their immorality threatened to lure the Israelites away from their covenant with God. In Deuteronomy 20:18, Moses warned the Israelites not to let the Canaanites live, for fear that they would *"persuade [the Israelites] to worship their disgusting gods."*

Thus, after Moses' death, Joshua led the people into battle many times as they sought to conquer the land God had promised them. Joshua's first obstacle was to capture the well-fortified city of Jericho. A heavenly messenger delivered the battle plan: The Israelites were to march around the city once a day for six days. On the seventh day, they were to march around the city seven times, sound their trumpets of war, then raise their voices in a mighty clamor. Bizarre as this sonic strategy must have sounded, Joshua did exactly as the messenger had instructed, until, as the old song tells us, "the walls came tumblin' down." (Find the story in Joshua 6.)

In another phenomenal event, the Israelites were pressing hard against a coalition of enemy armies, but they were quickly losing daylight. Soon their enemies would be able to escape into the darkness. Joshua looked skyward and said, *"Our Lord, make the sun stop in the sky over Gibeon, and the moon stand still over Aijalon Valley"* (Joshua 10:12). In response to his prayer, we are told, *"the sun stood still and didn't go down for about a whole day"* (Joshua 10:13). As if to emphasize the weight of that statement, the next verse says, *"Never before and never since has the Lord done anything like that for someone who prayed."*

A message from
THE BIBLE

JOSHUA 6:2–5

The Lord said to Joshua:

With my help, you and your army will defeat the king of Jericho and his army, and you will capture the town. Here is how to do it: March slowly around Jericho once a day for six days. Take along the sacred chest and have seven priests walk in front of it, carrying trumpets.

But on the seventh day, march slowly around the town seven times while the priests blow their trumpets. Then the priests will blast on their trumpets, and everyone else will shout. The wall will fall down, and your soldiers can go straight in from every side.

The oasis of Jericho in Israel blooms against the surrounding desert. The horns of Jericho were sounded during Joshua's conquest (Joshua 2:1).

WHAT'S THE POINT? **ENDURE . . . SO YOU CAN REST**

God promised to give the Israelites rest after they conquered Canaan (Deuteronomy 12:10). Thus Joshua is seen as the man responsible for leading Israel into its promised rest.

This concept of rest occurs throughout the Bible. According to Joshua 11:23, the Israelites did, in fact, enjoy a time of "peace" (or "rest," as some Bible versions put it) after they had subdued the Canaanites. The Israelites may have seen a connection between Israel's rest and the rest enjoyed by God after he created the universe (see Genesis 1:1—2:4).

The New Testament picks up on this theme, presenting Jesus as a second Joshua, leading his followers into an even greater rest. Joshua's rest was only a shadow of the real thing, according to the author of Hebrews. Christians may be called to endure hardship—much like the Israelites endured combat—all the while remembering Jesus' promise to lead his people into *"a Sabbath when we will rest"* (Hebrews 4:8–10).

the battles of
SAMSON

The Israelites' long-awaited settlement of the promised land of Canaan did not always go smoothly. They prospered at times, but the power of their armies always reflected the power of their faith; when their love of God diminished, they often fell under the sway of their enemies. In one such period, the Israelites were ruled by one of their fiercest rivals, the Philistines, for more than forty years. An angel of the Lord announced to Manoah and his wife, a Hebrew couple, that, despite their previous inability to conceive a child, they would give birth to a son. When the child was born, his mother named him Samson, a name derived from a Hebrew word that means "sun." (Read Judges 13:2–5.)

Samson's parents were told that their son was to be raised as a Nazirite, an ascetic sect of the Israelites, and would be required to take an ancient vow of intense spiritual dedication. As a symbol of his commitment to the ways of the Nazirites, Samson was never to cut his hair. His long, flowing locks would be a sign that the boy had been set apart by God for a great purpose.

While the Philistines ruled Israel with a stern hand, Samson grew in strength—and his strength kept increasing. Samson married a Philistine woman, and after being deceived by his father-in-law, Samson executed revenge by catching 300 foxes, pairing them up, and tying torches to their tails. Then he set the foxes free to run through the Philistines' fields, burning their crops to the ground. The Philistines sought revenge on Samson, but Samson ended up killing 1,000 of them with the jawbone of a donkey. (Read Judges 15:1–20.) Samson seemed unstoppable.

The Philistines could not hope to outfight Samson, nor could they discover the secret of his strength (which was his long hair and the vow it represented). So the Philistines offered a woman named Delilah 1,100 pieces of silver to discover Samson's secret. She succeeded. While Samson slept in her lap, Delilah clipped one long-flowing lock after another, until his hair (and his strength) was gone. Samson awoke to find himself surrounded and helpless. The Philistines gouged out his eyes and put him to work in their mills.

Samson's enemies seemed to take little notice as his hair grew and his strength returned. When they paraded their captive in front of an enormous crowd in their temple, Samson took his revenge: he pushed against the building's pillars until they fell and the temple collapsed, killing Samson and his enemies. Samson's captors had solved the mystery of his great strength, but they had overlooked its true source: his vow to serve God. (Read all about Samson in Judges 13–16.)

A message from
THE BIBLE

JUDGES 16:28–30
Samson prayed, "Please remember me, LORD God. The Philistines poked out my eyes, but make me strong one last time, so I can take revenge for at least one of my eyes!"

Samson was standing between the two middle columns that held up the roof [of the Philistine temple]. He felt around and found one column with his right hand, and the other with his left hand.

Then he shouted, "Let me die with the Philistines!" He pushed against the columns as hard as he could, and the temple collapsed with the Philistine rulers and everyone else still inside. Samson killed more Philistines when he died than he had killed during his entire life.

Samson fought the Philistines near these hills between Beth-Shemesh and Jerusalem (Judges 15:16).

WHAT'S THE POINT? **TRAGIC HERO**

Samson's story reads like that of a tragic hero. One scholar likens him to a star athlete whose off-the-field antics overshadow his professional achievements.

At a deeper level, Samson reveals something about the nation as a whole. He epitomizes Israel's sorry state, as detailed in the book of Judges. Like Samson, the Israelites squandered their God-given advantages, choosing instead to go their own way. Both Samson and the Israelites seemed to think they were accountable to no one. As the writer of Judges observed, *"Everyone did what they thought was right"* (21:25). Some scholars think Samson's story—and the larger story of Judges—was written to demonstrate Israel's need for a righteous king who would point the people back to God.

the battles of
DAVID

David is one of the Old Testament's renowned heroes, a humble shepherd who became one of Israel's greatest kings. While Joshua commanded entire armies, early on in his military career, David was more a guerrilla fighter, leading a small band of warriors who hid from the enemy, only to strike unexpectedly in small, deadly skirmishes. David's first conflict is one of the Bible's most memorable combats: as the armies of the Israelites and the Philistines looked on, the shepherd boy slew the enemy's champion, the giant Goliath, with a single stone from his slingshot. This triumph was followed by a skillful skein of victories that inspired a taunting chant directed at King Saul: *"Saul has killed a thousand enemies; David has killed ten thousand!"* Hearing this, Saul became intensely jealous of David. (Read 1 Samuel 18:7–8.)

There was a deeper significance to David's military successes. They showed that he, not Saul, was God's choice for king of Israel. Saul had failed in his kingly duties. Therefore, at God's direction, the prophet Samuel sought out David and anointed him as Saul's successor. (Read 1 Samuel 16:1–13.) Despite his success, David believed he should let God decide when he would assume the throne. Until then, David remained loyal to King Saul.

In the meantime, Saul sought to capture and kill David, so the young warrior slipped away to the wilderness and formed a small ragtag army. Staying out of sight, he moved from cave to cave with his band of guerrillas. Saul was unnerved to discover that David had twice doubled back on him, penetrated his camp, and stood close enough to kill him—yet hadn't done so. (Read 1 Samuel 24 and 26.)

David was a clever strategist. While avoiding Saul's soldiers, he sought refuge for more than a year where least expected: in the ranks of Israel's greatest enemy, the Philistines. He would trick the Philistine king into believing that he was fighting the Israelites, when he was really attacking the king's own Philistine settlements! David's survival depended on his ability to convince the Philistines that they might enlist his help against Israel, while seeing to it that he never raised a hand against his homeland. (Read 1 Samuel 27.)

It was a double life—one of patient endurance combined with disguise, deceit, and subterfuge. Through it all, David's close relationship with God sustained him. Years later, however, David's skill at deception would be his undoing, when his affair with Bathsheba and treacherous cover-up nearly cost him the throne (See 2 Samuel 11 and 12).

A message from
THE BIBLE

2 SAMUEL 22:1–4

David sang a song to the Lord after the Lord had rescued him from his enemies, especially Saul. These are the words to David's song:

Our Lord and our God,
you are my mighty rock,
    my fortress, my protector.
You are the rock
    where I am safe.
You are my shield,
my powerful weapon,
    and my place of shelter.
You rescue me and keep me
    safe from violence.
I praise you, our Lord!
    I prayed to you,
and you rescued me
    from my enemies.

This spring in the Cave of En-Gedi waters the region that descends to the Red Sea. Here David hid from a vengeful King Saul.

WHAT'S THE POINT? **GOD'S DELIVERER**

David was a complicated figure. On the one hand, his violent ways cost him the privilege of building a temple for God. (That honor fell to his son Solomon; see 1 Chronicles 22:6–10.) On the other hand, David delivered his people from their oppressors, the Philistines, and successfully established Israel's kingdom as a united monarchy. For his devotion to God, David was promised an everlasting dynasty (2 Samuel 7:1–17).

Thus David's perseverance on the battlefield paved the way for another deliverer: Jesus. The New Testament presents Jesus as David's true heir, the fulfillment of God's promise that a son of David would always rule (Luke 1:30–33).

WHAT WAS JESUS' MISSION?

Who Was He? Why Did He Come?

The New Testament presents Jesus as the Messiah, God in the flesh. For Christians, his identity—and the deeper meaning behind it—is a paradox. Jesus, according to the Bible, is both fully God and fully human. He is God's Son, and yet he came to earth as a person.

The true meaning of who Jesus is has been the subject of intense study over the centuries. Jesus' life began ordinarily enough (apart from his miraculous birth). His was a fully human experience. His father was a carpenter (Matthew 13:55), which at that time probably implied a builder who worked not only with wood but with a variety of materials. Apparently, Jesus followed in his father's footsteps, becoming a carpenter, too—at first, that is (Mark 6:3).

As Jesus entered adulthood, his life took on new meaning. He began speaking in the synagogues of Galilee, amazing people with his authoritative teaching. He attracted followers, and rumors began swirling around him. Was this the long-awaited Messiah—the promised deliverer, the son of David who had come to reclaim Israel's throne? The fact that Jesus chose twelve disciples likely fueled speculation. Not many first-century Jews would have missed the significance of a descendant of David with twelve followers; they would have presumed Jesus had come to liberate the twelve tribes of Israel.

The controversy surrounding Jesus' identity and mission put him on a crash course with the religious establishment: Jesus did not conform to their expectations. During his many confrontations with his opponents, Jesus left them dumbstruck, impressing those who saw and heard the exchanges (Luke 4:31–32). A central theme of Jesus' controversial message was that true honor comes from serving others, not from elevating oneself.

MEETING JESUS

We know from the Bible that Jesus fully understood the human experience. We can paint a further probable picture of his life from what we now know of the usual customs and typical experiences of a Jewish man in the Roman province of Judea.

Jesus' extended family would have been as much a part of his life as his immediate family. He was raised to honor his parents, and the responsibility to care for them in their old age would have been emphasized as he grew up. As a young man, he would have been trained at home and at the synagogue, studying the Law of Moses.

He probably ate two meals a day, at noon and at the end of the day. The menu may have included bread, vegetables, fruit, fish, and milk products, including yogurt and cheese. Meat was a luxury item.

Jesus would have slept on a mat on the floor beside other family members. He would have attended large weddings and feasts with them as well. Among his family, hospitality, even to strangers, would have been highly valued.

He likely had a beard and longer hair than his Greek and Roman counterparts. He would have worn a tunic, a knee-length garment made of linen. It would have been tied around his waist with a sash. For cooler days, he probably added a cloak, perhaps made of wool.

His was a culture in which identity was founded more in the group than in the individual. A person's family and nationality were essential aspects of his or her life. On an individual basis, the esteem of one's fellow citizens determined a person's sense of honor or shame. What wealth is to modern capitalist cultures, honor was to the first-century Mediterranean culture.

WHAT'S THE POINT?

The idea that Jesus was a real, flesh-and-blood human is essential to understanding the New Testament's portrait of him. According to the writer of Hebrews, it was only because of his genuine humanity that Jesus could relate to his fellow human beings and rescue them from sin (see Hebrews 4:14–16).

Head of Christ
17th century. Oil on wood panel.
Attributed to Rembrandt (1606–1669)

WHO DO YOU SAY THAT I AM?

According to the New Testament, mere humanity was not all there was to Jesus' identity. Jesus spoke with authority that inspired the masses. Not only did he stir hearts, but he transformed lives. Jesus' words healed the sick and even raised the dead.

These inspired acts reinforced the idea that Jesus is God. Sometimes the New Testament authors made this claim quite directly, such as when Paul wrote that *"God lives fully in Christ"* (Colossians 2:9). Other writers were more subtle, yet they left unmistakable clues about the deeper meaning of Jesus' identity. For example, the Gospel writer John mentioned seven miraculous signs performed by Jesus, as well as seven "I am" statements uttered by him. John's Jewish readers would not have missed the significance of the number seven, often associated with the divine, or Jesus' frequent use of God's most personal name, "I Am" (see page 60).

Subtle or straightforward, Jesus' divine nature is central to the New Testament portrayal of him. As stated in Colossians 1:15: *"Christ is exactly like God, who cannot be seen. He is the first-born Son, superior to all creation."*

A message from
THE BIBLE

JOHN 1:1

In the beginning was the one who is called the Word.
The Word was with God and was truly God.

"I AM TRYING HERE TO PREVENT ANYONE SAYING THE REALLY FOOLISH THING THAT PEOPLE OFTEN SAY ABOUT HIM: 'I'M READY TO ACCEPT JESUS AS A GREAT MORAL TEACHER, BUT I DON'T ACCEPT HIS CLAIM TO BE GOD.' THAT IS THE ONE THING WE MUST NOT SAY. A MAN WHO WAS MERELY A MAN AND SAID THE SORT OF THINGS JESUS SAID WOULD NOT BE A GREAT MORAL TEACHER. HE WOULD EITHER BE A LUNATIC — ON A LEVEL WITH THE MAN WHO SAYS HE IS A POACHED EGG — OR ELSE HE WOULD BE THE DEVIL OF HELL. YOU MUST MAKE YOUR CHOICE. EITHER THIS MAN WAS, AND IS, THE SON OF GOD: OR ELSE A MADMAN OR SOMETHING WORSE. YOU CAN SHUT HIM UP FOR A FOOL, YOU CAN SPIT AT HIM AND KILL HIM AS A DEMON; OR YOU CAN FALL AT HIS FEET AND CALL HIM LORD AND GOD. BUT LET US NOT COME WITH ANY PATRONIZING NONSENSE ABOUT HIS BEING A GREAT HUMAN TEACHER. HE HAS NOT LEFT THAT OPEN TO US. HE DID NOT INTEND TO."

—Source: *Mere Christianity* written by C.S. Lewis (1952, Macmillan/Collier).

TEACHING, MISSION, and REVOLUTION

Jesus taught much about the kingdom of God. His message, like John the Baptist's, was an urgent call for each of us to repent of our sins—not because the kingdom of God was coming eventually, but because the kingdom of God had already come. But the true meaning of his message was often missed. Many were looking for an earthly kingdom to be established at a given time and place. Yet the kingdom Jesus preached was offering something different.

A message from THE BIBLE

MATTHEW 13:44–46

The kingdom of heaven is like what happens when someone finds a treasure hidden in a field and buries it again. Such a person is happy and goes and sells everything in order to buy that field.

The kingdom of heaven is like what happens when a shop owner is looking for fine pearls. After finding a very valuable one, the owner goes and sells everything in order to buy that pearl.

Jesus had not come to make Israel politically victorious over its enemies. He had not come to reign over a nation with the royal trappings of an army and castle. He had come to serve, to suffer, and to sacrifice himself (Matthew 20:28). He had come to show humanity how to live as members of God's kingdom (Matthew 5:2–12).

While the true nature of Jesus' mission caught many by surprise, it was deeply rooted in the preceding storyline of the Bible. The Old Testament prophet Isaiah had promised a deliverer who would suffer and sacrifice rather than conquer. Isaiah envisioned a Messiah who would be *"wounded and crushed,"* who would endure painful abuse without complaint (Isaiah 53).

Jesus' life and teaching were revolutionary because he defied popular but misguided notions of what the kingdom of God should look like. He preached a message that countered the status quo of his culture. Though he honored the commandments of God and many of the traditions of his people, like the ancient prophets before him, he seemed to abhor those who practiced religion for religion's sake, by rote or for show. He confronted the hypocrisy of some of the religious leaders and openly disregarded traditions that were inconsistent with the spirit of the law (Matthew 23:1–36).

And most revolutionary of all, as Jesus' ministry progressed, he revealed more and more of his true identity—showing that he was the promised Messiah. In other words, he was truly Immanuel, which means *"God is with us"* (Mathew 1:23).

Parable of the Hidden Treasure, c. 1630
Rembrandt

Christ Crowned with Thorns
20th-century wood. Filipino School
Boltin Picture Library/The Bridgeman Art Library

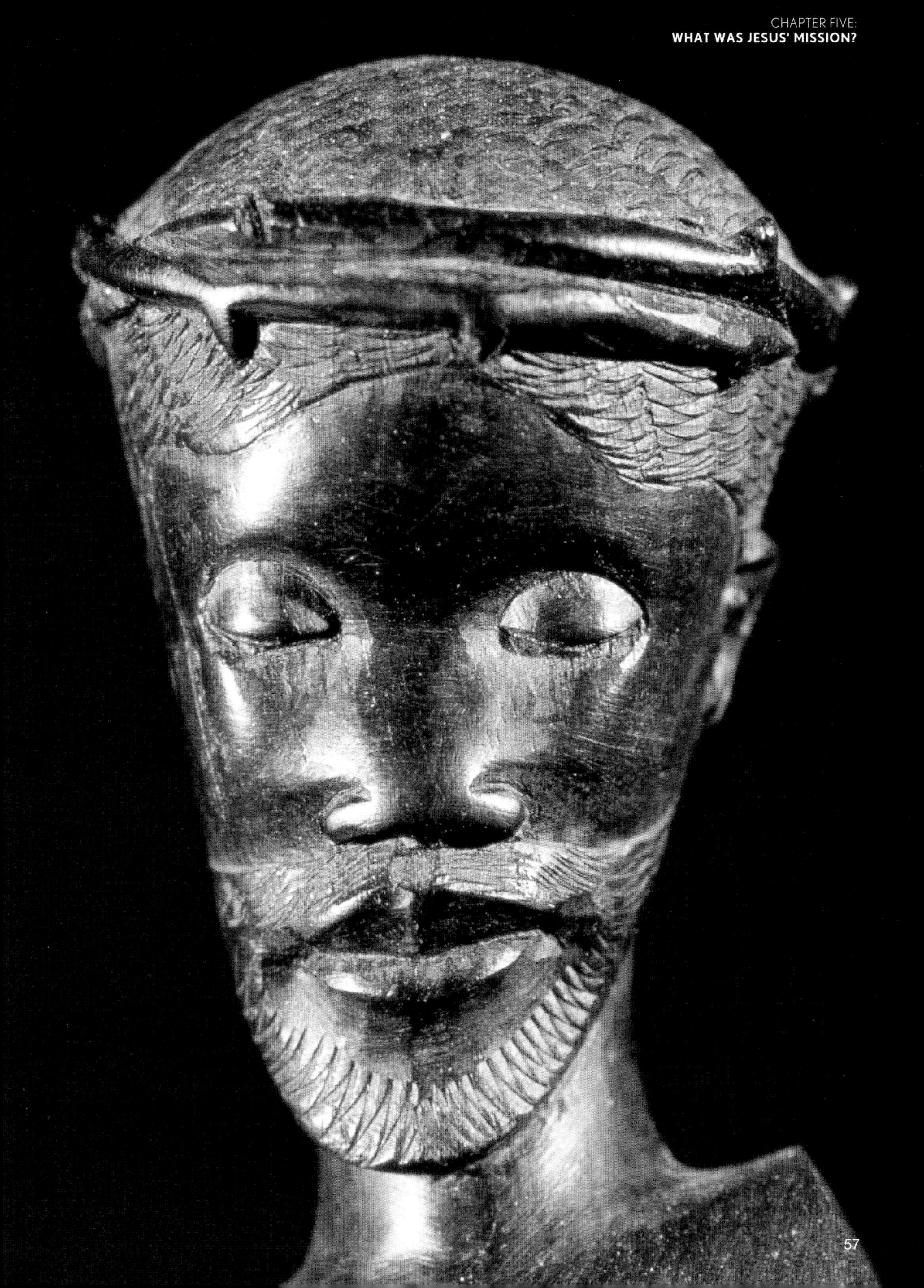

PROPHECIES, MIRACLES, and HEALED LIVES

Jesus' life was filled with wonders and miracles. Certain details of his life were connected to ancient prophecies written or spoken centuries before Jesus lived. He proved his power over nature by calming storms (Mark 4:35–41); over death by disrupting funerals and even grave sites to bring people back to life (Mark 5:35–43; John 11:17–44); over sickness by bringing health (Mark 5:25–34). The intended significance of these miracles was to reveal God's glory and to say, in essence: This is the One of whom the ancient prophets spoke, the promised deliverer who was to come at the climax of Israel's story.

While Jesus desired faith from his followers that did not rely on his miracles, they played an important part in revealing his authority as God's Son.

An Old Testament prophecy is found in Isaiah 35:3–6 that Jesus' followers applied to Jesus and to the good he would bring to those who believed in him:

*Here is a message for all
who are weak, trembling,
 and worried:
"Cheer up! Don't be afraid.
Your God is coming
 to punish your enemies.*

*God will take revenge on them
 and rescue you."*

*The blind will see,
and the ears of the deaf
 will be healed.
Those who were lame
 will leap around like deer;
tongues once silent
 will shout for joy.
Water will rush
 through the desert.*

A message from THE BIBLE

MATTHEW 11:2–6

John was in prison when he heard what Christ was doing. So John sent some of his followers to ask Jesus, "Are you the one we should be looking for? Or must we wait for someone else?"

Jesus answered, "Go and tell John what you have heard and seen. The blind are now able to see, and the lame can walk. People with leprosy are being healed, and the deaf can hear. The dead are raised to life, and the poor are hearing the good news. God will bless everyone who doesn't reject me because of what I do."

Salome with the Head of John the Baptist, c. 1607
Caravaggio, National Gallery, London

Christ Before Pilate
Undated. Pastel
Walter Beck (1864–1954)
Smithsonian American Art Museum, Washington, DC

THE GREAT "I AM" SAYINGS

Toward the end of his Gospel, John revealed his true purpose for writing: *"Jesus worked many other miracles for his disciples, and not all of them are written in this book. But these are written so that you will put your faith in Jesus as the Messiah and the Son of God. If you have faith in him, you will have true life"* (John 20:30–31).

John's aim was twofold. On one hand, he sought to demonstrate that Jesus is *"the Messiah and the Son of God."* On the other, he wanted people to know the true meaning of Jesus' identity so they could *"have life, and have it fully"* (John 10:10).

John alluded to Jesus' identity through two simple words: "I am." Seven times he quoted Jesus using this phrase, and Jesus' use of these words was anything but arbitrary.

When God commanded Moses to lead Israel out of slavery in Egypt, Moses asked for God's name. God replied, *"Tell them that the LORD, whose name is 'I Am,' has sent you"* (Exodus 3:13–15). Jesus showed that he had been in God's plan from the beginning when he said, *"Even before Abraham was, I was, and I am"* (John 8:58).

In John's Gospel, Jesus uses the term "I am" to connect himself to aspects of God's nature and to identify himself as the one who

- supplies all needs;
- brings the knowledge about God to all people;
- is the way for people to find God and become God's people;
- promises that all who believe in him will have eternal life;
- invites everyone to share in the common life as the new people of God.

I AM THE BREAD THAT GIVES LIFE!

JOHN 6:47-51

I tell you for certain that everyone who has faith in me has eternal life.

I am the bread that gives life! Your ancestors ate manna in the desert, and later they died. But the bread from heaven has come down, so that no one who eats it will ever die. I am that bread from heaven! Everyone who eats it will live forever. My flesh is the life-giving bread I give to the people of this world.

I AM THE LIGHT FOR THE WORLD!

JOHN 8:12

Once again Jesus spoke to the people. This time he said, "I am the light for the world! Follow me, and you won't be walking in the dark. You will have the light that gives life."

I AM THE GATE FOR THE SHEEP.

JOHN 10:7-10

Jesus said: "I tell you for certain that I am the gate for the sheep. Everyone who came before me was a thief or a robber, and the sheep did not listen to any of them. I am the gate. All who come in through me will be saved. Through me they will come and go and find pasture. A thief comes only to rob, kill, and destroy. I came so everyone would have life, and have it fully."

I AM THE GOOD SHEPHERD.

JOHN 10:11-16

I am the good shepherd, and the good shepherd gives up his life for his sheep. Hired workers are not like the shepherd. They don't own the sheep, and when they see a wolf coming, they run off and leave the sheep. Then the wolf attacks and scatters the flock. Hired workers run away because they don't care about the sheep.

I am the good shepherd. I know my sheep, and they know me. Just as the Father knows me, I know the Father, and I give up my life for my sheep. I have other sheep that are not in this sheep pen. I must also bring them together, when they hear my voice. Then there will be one flock of sheep and one shepherd.

I AM THE ONE WHO RAISES THE DEAD TO LIFE!

JOHN 11:25-27

Jesus then said [to Martha], "I am the one who raises the dead to life! Everyone who has faith in me will live, even if they die. And everyone who lives because of faith in me will never really die. Do you believe this?"

"Yes, Lord!" she replied. "I believe you are Christ, the Son of God. You are the one we hoped would come into the world."

I AM THE WAY, THE TRUTH, AND THE LIFE!

JOHN 14:6

I am the way, the truth, and the life! . . . Without me, no one can go to the Father.

I AM THE VINE.

JOHN 15:5-7

I am the vine, and you are the branches. If you stay joined to me, and I stay joined to you, then you will produce lots of fruit. But you cannot do anything without me. If you don't stay joined to me, you will be thrown away. You will be like dry branches that are gathered up and burned in a fire.

Stay joined to me and let my teachings become part of you. Then you can pray for whatever you want, and your prayer will be answered.

The Tomb of Lazarus at Jerusalem
Anonymous, 19th century

SUPERNATURAL MEANING behind SUPERNATURAL POWER

Jesus' miracles may be the most-beloved and best-remembered aspects of his time on earth. Jesus was a great healer. But what was the meaning behind these extraordinary feats of power and compassion?

Many believe the Old Testament prophet Isaiah foretold the miracles of the person whom Jews thought would be the Messiah: giving sight to the blind, enabling the deaf to hear, and making the lame walk. According to the Gospels, Jesus did all this and more. He healed the mute, the sick, victims of leprosy, and he even brought people back from the dead. For Jesus' followers, these miracles were more than just proof of his power; they connected him to the promises of Isaiah. They were a testimony to his identity as Messiah and Son of God. Indeed, some witnesses to the good news of Jesus' miracles went to John the Baptist as he languished in prison and assured him that the signs and wonders performed by Jesus testified that Jesus was, in fact, the Messiah for whom they had been waiting.

ONE STORY

The significance of Jesus' miracles should be understood in light of the individual Gospel accounts. Each Gospel was written with a different audience and purpose in mind.

MATTHEW

Matthew wrote to a Jewish audience to represent Jesus as the Messiah foretold in the Old Testament. He includes the miracles of Jesus to help with that representation, and he emphasizes the responses of the people who witnessed the miracles.

MARK

Mark represents Jesus' miracles not as those that lead to faith but that come from faith. Therefore, his account highlights the faith of those interacting with Jesus and receiving blessings from the miracles he performs.

LUKE

Luke's Gospel was written to provide a detailed account of Jesus' life. He emphasizes Jesus' compassion for the sick and the poor, and he connects Jesus' miracles more to the work of the Holy Spirit (see also Acts 10:38).

JOHN

John's Gospel was written so that the readers of that Gospel would believe in Jesus and thus receive true life. This Gospel includes seven miracles that function as signs that introduce the teachings of Jesus and emphasize his unique authority.

FOUR PERSPECTIVES

WHY MIRACLES?

Supernatural phenomena are by nature impossible to comprehend. Yet even if the New Testament doesn't explain *how* miracles were performed, it sheds some light on *why* they were performed.

RESPONSE TO FAITH For the most part, Jesus healed those who demonstrated faith in his power. In several accounts, there seems to be a vital relationship between the miracle performed and the faith of its beneficiary. In fact, Jesus was unable to perform many miracles in his own hometown due to his neighbors' *lack of faith* (Mark 6:1–6). As Jesus reminded onlookers before he restored Lazarus to life, seeing God's glory requires faith (John 11:40).

REWARD FOR PERSISTENCE In one instance, a Canaanite woman persistently followed Jesus, declaring her faith and asking him to heal her daughter, who was possessed by demons. The disciples were annoyed by the woman's persistence; even Jesus seemed to dismiss her at first. Yet this did not stop her from begging Jesus to help. Jesus finally answered her: *"Dear woman, you really do have a lot of faith, and you will be given what you want."* At that moment her daughter was healed (Matthew 15:28).

INVITATION TO BELIEVE As Jesus' reputation as a miracle worker grew, more crowds approached him with their sick and disabled (Matthew 15:29–31). Some begged just for a chance to touch his clothes, and all who touched his garment were healed (Matthew 14:34–36; Mark 6:53–56). And as people witnessed Jesus' miracles or heard of his great works, many put their faith in him. John concludes his Gospel by noting that he could hardly give an exhaustive account of Jesus' miracles. Nevertheless, he included several miraculous stories precisely so *"you will put your faith in Jesus as the Messiah and the Son of God"* (John 20:30–31).

WARNING AGAINST UNBELIEF The Gospels tell us that those who witnessed Jesus' miracles but lacked faith received harsh words of impending judgment (Matthew 11:20–24; Luke 10:13–16). Jesus' miracles were not an end unto themselves; they served to announce the kingdom of God and the restoration of a right relationship with God.

A message from THE BIBLE

ISAIAH 35:5–6

The blind will see,
and the ears of the deaf
   will be healed.
Those who were lame
   will leap around like deer;
tongues once silent
   will shout for joy.
Water will rush
   through the desert.

MATTHEW 11:4–6

Jesus answered, "Go and tell John what you have heard and seen. The blind are now able to see, and the lame can walk. People with leprosy are being healed, and the deaf can hear. The dead are raised to life, and the poor are hearing the good news. God will bless everyone who doesn't reject me because of what I do."

JOHN 21:25

Jesus did many other things. If they were all written in books, I don't suppose there would be room enough in the whole world for all the books.

Jesus Healing Peter's Mother-in-Law, c. 1020
Hitda Evangelary, Darmstadt

TURNING WATER INTO WINE

Jesus, who gradually became well known for healing the sick and raising the dead, performed his first miracle (as recorded by John) at a wedding feast in the village of Cana, where he turned water into wine to save the bridegroom's family from humiliation.

Jesus, along with his mother Mary and his disciples, was a guest at the celebration when the hosts ran out of wine. In a society that valued hospitality so highly, such an embarrassment threatened to tarnish the host family's reputation for years. Mary sprang into action, alerting Jesus to the situation and instructing the servants to do whatever he told them.

Jesus had the servants fill six very large stone jars with water, each holding twenty to thirty gallons. Then he told them to take a sample to the banquet host. The host drank the water, only it was not water but wine—and wine of exceptional quality, too. The host called the bridegroom over and expressed his amazement that he had saved the best wine until the end of the feast when it was customary to serve lower-quality wine. (Read the full account in John 2:1–12.)

This miracle not only saved a family's reputation, it connected Jesus to one of the most important symbols in the Bible. Wine was often an image of divine blessing. The connection between Jesus and wine may have been John's way of telling his readers that Jesus was the very embodiment of God's abundant blessing.

left: *The Wedding Feast of Cana*
[Paolo] Veronese (1528–1588)

upper right: **Terracotta Roman jugs from Cana, Israel**
Studium Biblicum Franciscanum, Jerusalem, Israel

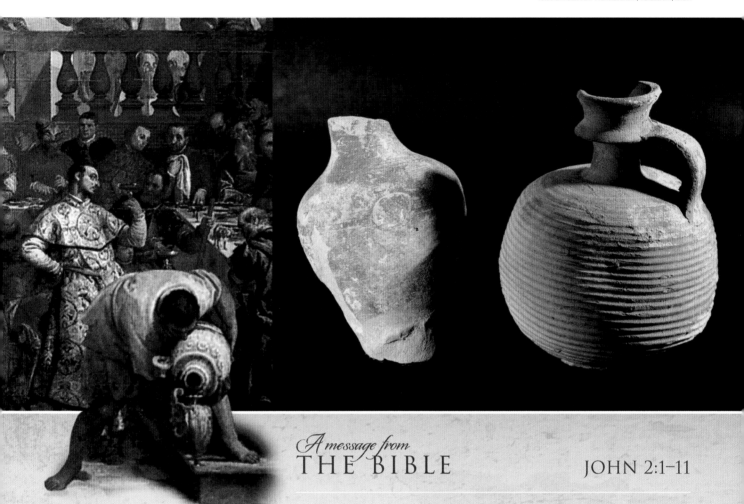

FOLLOW THE SIGNS

The Gospel writers included their accounts of the miracles of Jesus, not as stand-alone events, but as documentation of Jesus' ministry. In the case of John's Gospel, the miracles recorded often served as signs to everyone around of Jesus' identity. In fact, the word used for miracle in this fourth Gospel is a Greek word translated as "sign." The author of this Gospel pointed to Jesus as the Son of God and recounted the miracles to confirm that identity.

A message from
THE BIBLE   JOHN 2:1–11

Three days later Mary, the mother of Jesus, was at a wedding feast in the village of Cana in Galilee. Jesus and his disciples had also been invited and were there.

When the wine was all gone, Mary said to Jesus, "They don't have any more wine."

Jesus replied, "Mother, my time hasn't yet come! You must not tell me what to do." Mary then said to the servants, "Do whatever Jesus tells you to do."

At the feast there were six stone water jars that were used by the people for washing themselves in the way that their religion said they must. Each jar held about 20 or 30 gallons. Jesus told the servants to fill them to the top with water. Then after the jars had been filled, he said, "Now take some water and give it to the man in charge of the feast."

The servants did as Jesus told them, and the man in charge drank some of the water that had now turned into wine. He did not know where the wine had come from, but the servants did. He called the bridegroom over and said, "The best wine is always served first. Then after the guests have had plenty, the other wine is served. But you have kept the best until last!"

This was Jesus' first miracle, and he did it in the village of Cana in Galilee. There Jesus showed his glory, and his disciples put their faith in him.

HEALING A CHRONIC ILLNESS

Sometimes the miraculous healing bestowed by Jesus hinged on the initiative of the receiver.

Matthew, Mark, and Luke tell the story of a woman who had been bleeding for twelve years. According to Leviticus 15:25–27, her condition rendered her ceremonially *"unclean"* and unfit to worship with other Jews. No one would dare touch her, because doing so would make them unclean as well.

Yet instead of giving in to despair, the woman clung to her faith in Jesus' healing touch. So when she found herself in a crowd of people following Jesus, she seized her opportunity. Reaching out just enough to touch the edge of Jesus' clothing, she was immediately healed. Jesus, who felt the *"power going out,"* asked who had touched him (Luke 8:46). The woman came forward and told her story. Impressed, Jesus declared that she had been healed because of her faith.

One of the deeper messages of this healing is the value of persistence and initiative when it comes to seeking God. The power of this woman's experience was not just in the healing she received but also in the decisive role her faith played.

Her story also reveals something about Jesus' character. He was not at all concerned by being touched by someone *"unclean."* He was more interested in making people whole. When the Gospel writers note that Jesus *"felt power going out from"* himself, he was not discharging power like a battery, but rather he healed people by drawing on what later theologians would define as his divinity. Jesus' example inspired his early followers like Peter, who demonstrated how the power of God was able to bring about healing (see Acts 3:1–10; 9:32–42); and those who came in contact with the apostle Paul were also healed (see Acts 19:12). Likewise, more recent Christians were inspired to follow Jesus' example, such as Mother Teresa, who devoted her life to serving the poor and terminally ill of Calcutta.

Mother Teresa (1910–1997)
Roman Catholic nun, founder of the Missionaries of Charity

Jesus Healing the Hemophiliac Woman
Early Christian mosaic, Ravenna, Italy

A message from
THE BIBLE

LUKE 8:43–48
(see also Matthew 9:20–22; Mark 5:25–34)

In the crowd was a woman who had been bleeding for twelve years. She had spent everything she had on doctors, but none of them could make her well. As soon as she came up behind Jesus and barely touched his clothes, her bleeding stopped.

"Who touched me?" Jesus asked.

While everyone was denying it, Peter said, "Master, people are crowding all around and pushing you from every side." But Jesus answered, "Someone touched me, because I felt power going out from me." The woman knew that she could not hide, so she came trembling and knelt down in front of Jesus. She told everyone why she had touched him and that she had been healed at once.

Jesus said to the woman, "You are now well because of your faith. May God give you peace!"

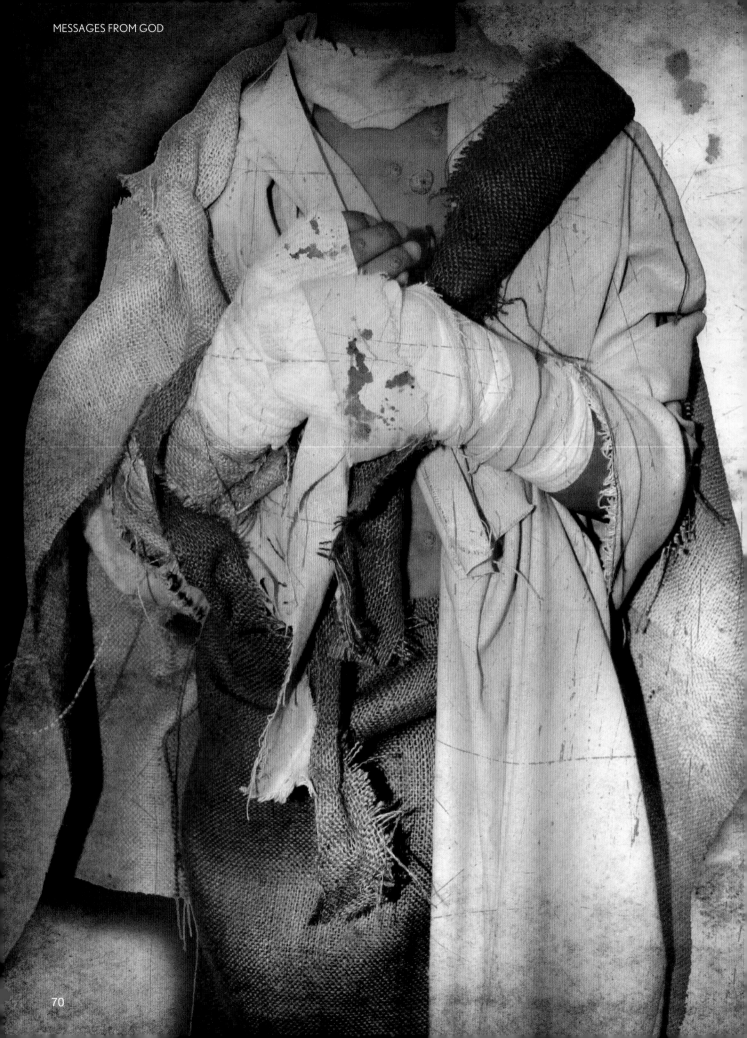

TOUCHING THE UNTOUCHABLE

Imagine being healed of a debilitating disease that had caused you to be cut off from society—only to be commanded not to tell anyone.

To have leprosy in the ancient world was to suffer a double fate. The disease not only ravaged the body; it severed a person's connection with their community. Lepers were required to tear their clothes, leave their hair uncombed, keep the lower part of their face covered, and shout, *"I'm unclean! I'm unclean!"* (Leviticus 13:45).

Despite his lowly status, one leper approached Jesus, kneeling before him and declaring that he believed Jesus had the power to make him well. According to Mark's Gospel account, Jesus took pity on the man, stretched out his hand and—to the surprise of everyone watching—touched him. According to the Law of Moses, touching the man should have made Jesus ritually unclean. Instead, Jesus' touch healed the man.

Jesus then commanded the man not to tell anyone about the miracle and to present himself to the priest in order to prove that he had been made well. Jesus' second command was a requirement according to the Law of Moses regarding the cleansing of lepers (see Leviticus 14:2–32).

But why keep the miracle a secret? Some scholars think it had to do with something called the "messianic secret." Jesus' popularity, fueled in part by miracles like this one, impeded his ability to move about freely. Messianic speculation was at a fever pitch, but Jesus knew he wouldn't be the kind of Messiah the crowds were looking for. Instead of ruling with an iron fist, he intended to serve with an open hand.

The Parable of Lazarus and Dives, c. 1035–1040
Illuminated manuscript, *Codex Aureus of Echternach*
Germanisches Nationalmuseum, Nuremberg

A message from THE BIBLE

MARK 1:40–45

(see also Matthew 8:1–4; Luke 5:12–16)

A man with leprosy came to Jesus and knelt down. He begged, "You have the power to make me well, if only you wanted to."

Jesus felt sorry for the man. So he put his hand on him and said, "I want to! Now you are well." At once the man's leprosy disappeared, and he was well.

After Jesus strictly warned the man, he sent him on his way. He said, "Don't tell anyone about this. Just go and show the priest that you are well. Then take a gift to the temple as Moses commanded, and everyone will know that you have been healed."

The man talked about it so much and told so many people, that Jesus could no longer go openly into a town. He had to stay away from the towns, but people still came to him from everywhere.

RAISING THE DEAD

Jesus turned his own grief into a powerful display of his authority over death.

Raising of Lazarus, 1304–1306
Giotto (c. 1267–1337)

Once Jesus was traveling with his disciples when news arrived that Lazarus, the brother of his close friends Mary and Martha, was ill.

Rather than rushing to the side of Lazarus in the village of Bethany, Jesus delayed his departure. Eventually, Lazarus died. It was another four days before Jesus came to his friend's house.

When Jesus arrived, some of the mourners wondered aloud why the famed healer hadn't prevented Lazarus' death. Overcome with emotion, Jesus approached the tomb and made an unusual request: he asked the people to roll away the stone.

As soon as the stone was moved, Jesus began to pray. Then he called out to the dead man they had buried and for whom they were grieving. According to John's Gospel account, Lazarus responded by walking out of the tomb, still wrapped in his burial clothes. Jesus had restored Lazarus to life!

Some experts see a deeper significance to the timing of Jesus' arrival. We are told that *"Lazarus had already been in the tomb four days"* (John 11:17). In the ancient world, when someone died, it wasn't possible to check their brain activity to pinpoint the moment of death. According to one ancient tradition, it was thought that a dead person's soul lingered near the body for three days. Beyond that, the possibility of resuscitation vanished, along with the deceased person's soul.

At four days, any last hope for Lazarus was as dead as he was. By waiting until then to act, Jesus sent an unforgettable message to followers and skeptics alike. He powerfully asserted his ability to bring new life and achieve victory over the grave.

A message from THE BIBLE   JOHN 11:38–44

Jesus was still terribly upset. So he went to the tomb, which was a cave with a stone rolled against the entrance. Then he told the people to roll the stone away. But Martha said, "Lord, you know that Lazarus has been dead four days, and there will be a bad smell."

Jesus replied, "Didn't I tell you that if you had faith, you would see the glory of God?"

After the stone had been rolled aside, Jesus looked up toward heaven and prayed, "Father, I thank you for answering my prayer. I know that you always answer my prayers. But I said this, so that the people here would believe that you sent me."

When Jesus had finished praying, he shouted, "Lazarus, come out!" The man who had been dead came out. His hands and feet were wrapped with strips of burial cloth, and a cloth covered his face.

Jesus then told the people, "Untie him and let him go."

FEEDING THOUSANDS

A message from
THE BIBLE

JOHN 6:1–14

*(see also Matthew 14:13–21; 15:32-39;
Mark 6:30–44; 8:1–10; Luke 9:10–17)*

Only one of Jesus' miracles is mentioned in every Gospel: the feeding of five thousand. What message was so important that all four Gospel writers included this story?

Each Gospel account paints a slightly different picture of the scene. Luke says the miracle occurred near the village of Bethsaida. Matthew reveals that Jesus healed many in the crowd just before feeding everyone.

Mark notes that the crowd was *"like sheep without a shepherd."* This was no mere turn of phrase. The Old Testament prophet Isaiah had promised God would come to rule his people—and that he would care for them *"as shepherds care for their flocks"* (Isaiah 40:10–11). Mark presents Jesus as the shepherd sent by God to feed his flock.

John shares an additional layer of meaning, connecting Jesus' miracle to another miraculous feeding. Centuries before Jesus, the wandering Israelites ate manna in the wilderness (see Exodus 16). After Jesus fed the five thousand, he reminded his listeners how God had fed their ancestors—and then declared himself to be *"the true bread from heaven,"* sent by God to nourish people everywhere (John 6:32–35).

This mosaic of the miracle of the loaves and fishes is located inside the church at Tabgha, Israel.

Jesus crossed Lake Galilee, which was also known as Lake Tiberias. A large crowd had seen him work miracles to heal the sick, and those people went with him. It was almost time for the Jewish festival of Passover, and Jesus went up on a mountain with his disciples and sat down. When Jesus saw the large crowd coming toward him, he asked Philip, "Where will we get enough food to feed all these people?" He said this to test Philip, since he already knew what he was going to do.

Philip answered, "Don't you know that it would take almost a year's wages just to buy only a little bread for each of these people?" Andrew, the brother of Simon Peter, was one of the disciples. He spoke up and said, "There is a boy here who has five small loaves of barley bread and two fish. But what good is that with all these people?" The ground was covered with grass, and Jesus told his disciples to tell everyone to sit down. About 5,000 men were in the crowd. Jesus took the bread in his hands and gave thanks to God. Then he passed the bread to the people, and he did the same with the fish, until everyone had plenty to eat.

The people ate all they wanted, and Jesus told his disciples to gather up the leftovers, so that nothing would be wasted. The disciples gathered them up and filled twelve large baskets with what was left over from the five barley loaves.

After the people had seen Jesus work this miracle, they began saying, "This must be the Prophet who is to come into the world!"

MASTERING THE STORM

Shortly after Jesus miraculously fed more than five thousand people, the disciples were caught in a mighty storm on Lake Galilee. What happened next forever changed their view of Jesus.

In the middle of the night, the winds kicked up and the waters grew choppy. As morning dawned, Jesus approached—walking on the water as if it were dry land! At first his disciples did not recognize him, but he revealed his identity, saying, *"Don't worry! I am Jesus. Don't be afraid"* (Matthew 14:27).

As Matthew tells the story, Peter responded, asking Jesus to call him out onto the water. Jesus obliged, and Peter stepped outside of the boat and began to walk across the waves toward Jesus. Quickly reminded of the fierce wind, Peter panicked and began to sink. In his desperation, Peter cried out to Jesus, who reached out and pulled him up. After Jesus brought Peter safely into the boat, the waters calmed.

At this point Matthew says the disciples worshiped Jesus—something they apparently hadn't done before. Their reaction offers a clue to the deeper significance of this story. To many in the ancient world, the sea was synonymous with the abyss—a place to be feared. Yet the opening chapter of Genesis hints at God's mastery over the chaotic seas: *"But the Spirit of God was moving over the water"* (1:2). In Matthew's Gospel, Jesus demonstrated the same mastery—not just in this story, when he walked on water and calmed the winds (14:22–33), but also earlier when he calmed a horrendous storm (8:23–27). The only explanation that made sense to the disciples was that they were standing in the presence of God incarnate.

left: ***Walking on Water***, 1888. Ivan Aivazovsky (1817–1900)
below: ***Jesus Takes Peter Who Failed to Walk on Water,*** 1411
Lluís Borrassà

A message from
THE BIBLE

MATTHEW 14:22–33

(see also Mark 6:45–52; John 6:16–21)

At once, Jesus made his disciples get into a boat and start back across the lake. But he stayed until he had sent the crowds away. Then he went up on a mountain where he could be alone and pray. Later in the evening, he was still there. By this time the boat was a long way from the shore. It was going against the wind and was being tossed around by the waves. A little while before morning, Jesus came walking on the water toward his disciples. When they saw him, they thought he was a ghost. They were terrified and started screaming.

At once, Jesus said to them, "Don't worry! I am Jesus. Don't be afraid." Peter replied, "Lord, if it is really you, tell me to come to you on the water."

"Come on!" Jesus said. Peter then got out of the boat and started walking on the water toward him.

But when Peter saw how strong the wind was, he was afraid and started sinking. "Save me, Lord!" he shouted.

At once, Jesus reached out his hand. He helped Peter up and said, "You surely don't have much faith. Why do you doubt?"

When Jesus and Peter got into the boat, the wind died down. The men in the boat worshiped Jesus and said, "You really are the Son of God!"

While you can find the same miracle of Jesus listed in more than one Gospel, often the details of the accounts are a little different. This is because each of the Gospels was written with a different purpose and audience in mind.

This account of Jesus walking on water is recorded in three Gospels—Matthew, Mark, and John (Matthew 14:22–33; Mark 6:45–52; John 6:16–21). Matthew's and Mark's versions differ only in that Matthew records Simon Peter also walking on the water and Jesus rescuing him. And true to Matthew's mission—to assure his Jewish readers that Jesus was the Messiah—he records the disciples' declaration that they recognized Jesus as the Son of God (Matthew 14:33).

John includes the detail that, after Jesus calmed the waves, the boat suddenly arrived at its destination (John 6:21). Since John wrote to encourage his readers to put their faith in Jesus, including this kind of detail supported his intent.

ILLUMINATING VISION?

The blinding light of the Transfiguration gave the disciples yet another clue as to Jesus' true identity.

top: Mount Tabor in Israel, traditionally identified as the Mount of Transfiguration

bottom: *Transfiguration* Raphael (1483 – 1520)

The story is recorded in three of the four Gospels—Matthew, Mark, and Luke. It took place six days after Jesus warned his disciples of his impending suffering and death. Jesus took Peter, James, and John with him up a mountain. There, he was transformed before their eyes; suddenly his face shone *"like the sun, and his clothes became white as light"* (Matthew 17:2).

To make the moment even more spectacular, Moses and Elijah, two of Israel's greatest prophets, suddenly appeared and began talking with Jesus.

As the disciples puzzled over this mysterious sight, a cloud descended; from it, the voice of God announced his approval of Jesus. The disciples, terrified at this display of God's presence, fell to the ground. Only after Jesus reassured them did they return to their feet.

Two details of the story—Jesus' shining face and the descending cloud—provide an important indication of what really took place on the mountain. In the book of Exodus, after Moses met with God on Mount Sinai, his face shone so brightly he had to wear a veil. Jesus' shining face, like Moses' before him, and Jesus' radiant clothing were an indication of his manifestation of the divine.

The descending cloud holds perhaps even greater significance to the story. When Solomon completed the first Jewish temple in 957 BC, God's presence was said to descend on the building in the form of a cloud (2 Chronicles 5:14). Centuries later, as Jerusalem fell, the prophet Ezekiel reported watching that same glory leave the temple (Ezekiel 10:18). The cloud that descended on Jesus and his disciples during the Transfiguration might have symbolized God's presence returning to his people—in the person of Jesus.

A message from
THE BIBLE

MATTHEW 17:1–9

(see also Mark 9:2–13; Luke 9:28–36; 2 Peter 1:16–18)

Six days later Jesus took Peter and the brothers James and John with him. They went up on a very high mountain where they could be alone. There in front of the disciples, Jesus was completely changed. His face was shining like the sun, and his clothes became white as light.

All at once Moses and Elijah were there talking with Jesus. So Peter said to him, "Lord, it is good for us to be here! Let us make three shelters, one for you, one for Moses, and one for Elijah."

While Peter was still speaking, the shadow of a bright cloud passed over them. From the cloud a voice said, "This is my own dear Son, and I am pleased with him. Listen to what he says!" When the disciples heard the voice, they were so afraid they fell flat on the ground. But Jesus came over and touched them. He said, "Get up and don't be afraid!" When they opened their eyes, they saw only Jesus.

On their way down from the mountain, Jesus warned his disciples not to tell anyone what they had seen until after the Son of Man had been raised from death.

Christ at the Column
Wood
Antonello da Messina (1430–1479)

FINDING MEANING IN DEATH

According to Genesis 3, death entered the world when Adam and Eve disobeyed God and ate the forbidden fruit. It has been an inescapable part of the human experience ever since. Yet for Christians, faith means believing that death does not have the last word. One of the great paradoxes of faith is the idea that the death of one man, Jesus, made it possible for those who believe in him to overcome death.

The day Jesus died, known as Good Friday, is one of the most sacred, solemn days on the Christian calendar. All four Gospels devote considerable attention to the circumstances of Jesus' crucifixion. But what deeper meaning lies behind the events leading up to and surrounding the death of Jesus? What can be discovered by retracing his steps to the cross on which he was executed? And why do millions of people place so much hope in the death of one man?

THE

SUNDAY*   MONDAY   TUESDAY   WEDNESDAY

Jesus' triumphal entry into Jerusalem

The next day a large crowd was in Jerusalem for Passover. When they heard that Jesus was coming for the festival, they took palm branches and went out to greet him. They shouted,

"Hooray! God bless the one who comes in the name of the Lord! God bless the King of Israel!"

(John 12:12–13)

While we do not know the actual days on which each event occurred, here is a traditional listing of events from the Passion Week.

Jesus runs the merchants out of the temple

When Jesus entered the temple, he started chasing out the people who were selling things. He told them, "The Scriptures say, 'My house should be a place of worship.' But you have made it a place where robbers hide!"

Each day, Jesus kept on teaching in the temple. So the chief priests, the teachers of the Law of Moses, and some other important people tried to have him killed. But they could not find a way to do it, because everyone else was eager to listen to him.

(Luke 19:45–48)

The conflicts in the temple

The Pharisees got together with Herod's followers. Then they sent some men to trick Jesus into saying something wrong. They went to him and said, "Teacher, we know that you are honest. You treat everyone with the same respect, no matter who they are. And you teach the truth about what God wants people to do. Tell us, should we pay taxes to the Emperor or not?" Jesus knew what they were up to, and he said, "Why are you trying to test me? Show me a coin!" They brought him a silver coin, and he asked, "Whose picture and name are on it?" "The Emperor's," they answered. Then Jesus told them, "Give the Emperor what belongs to him and give God what belongs to God." The men were amazed at Jesus.

(Mark 12:13–17)

The Plot for Jesus' death grows

It was now two days before Passover and the Festival of Thin Bread. The chief priests and the teachers of the Law of Moses were planning how they could sneak around and have Jesus arrested and put to death. They were saying, "We must not do it during the festival, because the people will riot."

(Mark 14:1–2)

TIMELINE
the events leading up to Easter

THURSDAY

Last Supper

Betrayal and arrest

Trial before Annas

Trial before Caiaphas

During the meal Jesus took some bread in his hands. He blessed the bread and broke it. Then he gave it to his disciples and said, "Take this and eat it. This is my body."

Jesus picked up a cup of wine and gave thanks to God. He then gave it to his disciples and said, "Take this and drink it. This is my blood, and with it God makes his agreement with you. It will be poured out, so that many people will have their sins forgiven."

(Matthew 26:26–28)

FRIDAY

Morning trial before the Sanhedrin

Trial before Pilate

Trial before Herod

Final trial before Pilate

Crucifixion and burial

Jesus knew that he had now finished his work. And in order to make the Scriptures come true, he said, "I am thirsty!" A jar of cheap wine was there. Someone then soaked a sponge with the wine and held it up to Jesus' mouth on the stem of a hyssop plant. After Jesus drank the wine, he said, "Everything is done!" He bowed his head and died.

(John 19:28–30)

SATURDAY

Jesus lies in the tomb

On the next day, which was a Sabbath, the chief priests and the Pharisees went together to Pilate. They said, "Sir, we remember what this liar said while he was still alive. He claimed in three days he would come back from death. So please order the tomb to be carefully guarded for three days. If you don't, his disciples may come and steal his body. They will tell the people he has been raised to life, and this last lie will be worse than the first one." Pilate said to them, "All right, take some of your soldiers and guard the tomb as well as you know how." So they sealed it tight and placed soldiers there to guard it.

(Matthew 27:62–66)

SUNDAY

Resurrection

The Sabbath was over, and it was almost daybreak on Sunday when Mary Magdalene and the other Mary went to see the tomb. Suddenly a strong earthquake struck, and the Lord's angel came down from heaven. He rolled away the stone and sat on it. The angel looked as bright as lightning, and his clothes were white as snow. The guards shook from fear and fell down, as though they were dead. The angel said to the women, "Don't be afraid! I know you are looking for Jesus, who was nailed to a cross. He isn't here! God has raised him to life, just as Jesus said he would. Come, see the place where his body was lying."

(Matthew 28:1–6)

PALM SUNDAY

Palm Sunday marked the start of Jesus' final week. On this day, Jesus entered Jerusalem at the height of popularity. Crowds met him, waving palm branches and shouting, *"Hosanna!"* (See Matthew 21:1–11; Mark 11:1–11; Luke 19:28–44; John 12:12–19.) What was the meaning behind the crowd's reaction? And how might it have angered the religious leaders who did not want to attract disapproval from the ruling Roman government?

**Everyone in Jerusalem,
   celebrate and shout!
Your king has won a victory,
   and he is coming to you.
He is humble
   and rides on a donkey;
he comes on the colt
   of a donkey.**

Zechariah 9:9

The Entry of Christ into Jerusalem, 1150
Mosaic
Cappella Palatina, Palermo, Italy

Many Christians believe the events of Palm Sunday fulfilled the prophecy found in Zechariah 9:9, in which a king comes to Jerusalem amid great rejoicing. He is pictured riding *"on a donkey."* Judging by the reaction to Jesus, the crowd that gathered around him certainly thought he had come to fulfill this prophecy.

In Jewish tradition, the palm branch was a symbol of triumph and of victory; it is treated as such in other parts of the Bible (see, for example, Leviticus 23:40 and Revelation 7:9). The word "Hosanna," shouted by the crowds as Jesus rode past, was an expression of joy at the prospect of deliverance; originally, it meant "Save us!"

Different Gospel accounts provide different details reinforcing the politically dangerous scene that is depicted. In Matthew, the crowd hails Jesus as *"the Son of David"* (21:9). Mark records them shouting, *"God bless the coming kingdom of our ancestor David"* (11:10). Perhaps the most provocative of them all, John remembers the crowd declaring that Jesus is *"the King of Israel"* (12:13).

This was not fuzzy sentiment on the crowd's part. At the time, Israel was under Roman rule. Many longed to see a Messiah rise up, lead them against their Roman oppressors, and reinstate the kingdom. Apparently, the crowd pressing in on Jesus thought he was poised to do just that.

How wrong they were. Already, the Jewish religious leaders were hatching a plan to have Jesus killed (see John 11:45–57). And as Jesus' followers would be shocked to discover, he had no intention of leading a military revolt against Israel's enemies.

A message from
THE BIBLE

MARK 11:1–11

Jesus and his disciples reached
Bethphage and Bethany
near the Mount of Olives. When
they were getting close to
Jerusalem, Jesus sent two of
them on ahead. He told them, "Go into
the next village. As soon as you enter it, you will find
a young donkey that has
never been ridden. Untie the donkey and bring
it here. If anyone asks why you are doing this, say,
'The Lord needs it and will soon bring it back.' "

The disciples left and found
the donkey tied near a door that
faced the street. While they were untying it, some
of the people standing there asked, "Why are you
untying the donkey?" They told them
what Jesus had said, and the people let them take it.

The disciples led the donkey to Jesus. They put
some of their clothes on its back, and Jesus got on.
Many people spread clothes on the road, while others
spread branches they had cut from the fields.

In front of Jesus and behind him, people
went along shouting,

"Hooray! God bless the one who comes in the name
of the Lord!

God bless the coming kingdom of our ancestor
David. Hooray for God in heaven above!"

After Jesus had gone to Jerusalem, he went into the
temple and looked around at everything. But since it
was already late in the day, he went back to Bethany
with the twelve disciples.

PREPARING A FEAST
Jesus' Last Passover Celebration

Jesus' final week unfolded against the backdrop of preparations for the Passover, a yearly festival that prompted many first-century Jews to travel to Jerusalem. The Passover feast, which commemorated God's dramatic rescue of the Israelites from bondage in Egypt, provided an important clue as to Jesus' real mission: it involved the sacrifice of an innocent lamb.

16th-century Orthodox fresco from Kremikovtsi

The origin of the Passover Festival is found in ancient Egypt, where the family of Jacob (also called Israel) sought refuge from a famine. There, over hundreds of years, that family grew into a nation of Israelite people enslaved by the Egyptians (Exodus 1:6–14). The Old Testament book of Exodus tells us that when Moses asked for the freedom of these enslaved people, God sent a series of plagues to convince Egypt's king to comply. In the last of these plagues, death swept across Egypt, taking the firstborn son of every family and firstborn male of all animals. Only the firstborn of those belonging to Israelite families were spared. As commanded by the Lord, they sacrificed an innocent lamb and marked their doorposts with the blood of that lamb so that the Lord's angel of death would pass over their homes (Exodus 12:21–23).

God instructed the people to commemorate the Passover yearly from then on. Each time a Jewish family celebrates the Passover, the children are invited to recount the story and all relive the event with a memorial meal.

Jesus, who anticipated his death (see Matthew 20:17–19; Mark 10:32–34; Luke 18:31–34), timed the decisive moment to coincide with the Passover Festival. His whole life seemed to be hurtling toward this moment, reinforcing his identity as the ultimate Passover Lamb, whose sacrifice has everlasting benefits. Years earlier, when Jesus was beginning his public ministry, John the Baptist called him *"the Lamb of God who takes away the sin of the world"* (John 1:29). And years later, the apostle Paul wrote, *"our Passover Lamb is Christ, who has already been sacrificed"* (1 Corinthians 5:7).

TELL THE PEOPLE OF ISRAEL

THAT ON THE TENTH DAY OF THIS MONTH THE HEAD OF EACH FAMILY MUST CHOOSE A LAMB OR A YOUNG GOAT FOR HIS FAMILY TO EAT. IF ANY FAMILY IS TOO SMALL TO EAT THE WHOLE ANIMAL, THEY MUST SHARE IT WITH THEIR NEXT-DOOR NEIGHBORS. CHOOSE EITHER A SHEEP OR A GOAT, BUT IT MUST BE A ONE-YEAR-OLD MALE THAT HAS NOTHING WRONG WITH IT. AND IT MUST BE LARGE ENOUGH FOR EVERYONE TO HAVE SOME OF THE MEAT.

EACH FAMILY MUST TAKE CARE OF ITS ANIMAL UNTIL THE EVENING OF THE FOURTEENTH DAY OF THE MONTH, WHEN THE ANIMALS ARE TO BE KILLED. SOME OF THE BLOOD MUST BE PUT ON THE TWO DOORPOSTS AND ABOVE THE DOOR OF EACH HOUSE WHERE THE ANIMALS ARE TO BE EATEN. THAT NIGHT THE ANIMALS ARE TO BE ROASTED AND EATEN, TOGETHER WITH BITTER HERBS AND THIN BREAD

THE THIEVES

As Jesus suffered on the cross that Friday, a microcosm of the world's reaction to his death unfolded beside him. Two criminals, sentenced to death for their crimes, endured their own prolonged ordeals along with him. The first, embittered by his physical pain and none-too-happy life, hurled sarcastic demands at Jesus: *"Aren't you the Messiah? Save yourself and save us!"* (Luke 23:39).

It isn't hard to understand such an attitude; the man beside him had been celebrated for raising people from the dead and walking on water. He had even claimed to be God's own Son. And now he seemed no different from the broken, powerless criminal who taunted him.

But the other thief presented an alternative to despair: he clung to his faith against all odds, in the very darkest hour of adversity. *"Don't you fear God?"* he asked. Those four words contained his belief. He turned toward Jesus and with reverence asked Jesus to remember him. And with compassion and authority in his voice, Jesus promised him paradise (Luke 23:40–43).

THE BURIAL OF JESUS

Jewish law required immediate burial for executed criminals; their bodies were not to be left on display overnight (see Deuteronomy 21:22–23). According to Matthew's Gospel, Joseph of Arimathea, a member of the Jewish Sanhedrin and a closet follower of Jesus, asked for the body so he could bury Jesus before nightfall. With Pilate's blessing, the Jewish religious leaders sealed the tomb and assigned soldiers to guard it (see Matthew 27:57–66).

The burial of Jesus is described briefly by Matthew and the other Gospel writers (see Mark 15:42–47; Luke 23:50–56; John 19:38–42), but it held great significance for early Christians. In two separate letters, the apostle Paul compared Jesus' burial to the act of baptism (see Romans 6:4 and Colossians 2:12). According to Paul, the path to victory runs through a tomb. New life cannot come without death; without Good Friday, there can be no Easter Sunday.

Top left: ***Crucifixion***, 1565
Tintoretto

Top right: ***A recreation of the burial place of Jesus***

Fresco at the wall of Moldovita Monastery
Bukovina, Romania

CH 8

the deeper meaning of the
RESURRECTION

Christian faith is an Easter faith, and Christians are also known as "Easter people." The resurrection of Jesus, celebrated by Christians on Easter Sunday, is the final seal on his message and his mission.

One of Jesus' noted followers, the apostle Paul (author of many of the New Testament letters), wrote that his faith would have no meaning apart from the reality of the resurrection. Jesus' resurrection was more than a singular event and is far more than the end of his story, for its deeper meaning is ongoing. It marks the beginning of a resurrection promised to those who follow Jesus and trust in his victory over death; it is a down payment guaranteeing God's ultimate triumph over evil.

The Christian message addresses the plight of humans when they choose their own way instead of God's way, a choice that results in both spiritual and physical death. Jesus' death was God's way of dealing with the captivity of humanity to sin and death. Jesus' resurrection was an emphatic message that his triumph over death can also be ours.

A message from
THE BIBLE
1 CORINTHIANS 15:12–22

If we preach that Christ was raised from death, how can some of you say the dead will not be raised to life? If they won't be raised to life, Christ himself wasn't raised to life. And if Christ wasn't raised to life, our message is worthless, and so is your faith. If the dead won't be raised to life, we have told lies about God by saying he raised Christ to life, when he really did not.

So if the dead won't be raised to life, Christ wasn't raised to life. Unless Christ was raised to life, your faith is useless, and you are still living in your sins. And those people who died after putting their faith in him are completely lost. If our hope in Christ is good only for this life, we are worse off than anyone else.

But Christ has been raised to life! And he makes us certain that others will also be raised to life. Just as we will die because of Adam, we will be raised to life because of Christ. Adam brought death to all of us, and Christ will bring life to all of us.

WISHFUL THINKING OR **REAL EVENT**?

While each of the four Gospels offers different details of the resurrection, they all report that the tomb was empty and Jesus was very much alive. Throughout the years, many theories have sought to explain the resurrection as a symbolic event only—or even as a case of outright fraud perpetrated by Jesus' followers. Yet the first Christians were convinced that Jesus physically rose from the dead. Without a resurrection, they argued, their faith would be meaningless. Many refused to recant, even to the point of death.

Below are a few of the theories about what happened, along with some points to consider that suggest the possibility that Jesus really did rise from the dead.

- **Jesus didn't really die on the cross. He merely fainted, then later was revived and went on his way.** Yet the soldiers who executed Jesus were professionals. They regularly oversaw the execution of criminals. Would they be that easily fooled?

- **The women simply went to the wrong tomb, one that was empty.** Yet this was not a modern cemetery with one identical grave site after another. The Bible states that the women noted the location of the tomb so they would be able to return (Matthew 27:61; Mark 15:47; Luke 23:55).

- **The disciples stole Jesus' body.** Unlikely, given the contingent of soldiers guarding the tomb (Matthew 27:62–66). Even many who doubt the resurrection accept the authenticity of the disciples' faith.

- **The disciples had visions of Jesus after his death, but his resurrection was spiritual, not physical.** In 1 Corinthians, Paul documents hundreds of witnesses who saw Jesus in the flesh, after his crucifixion (15:5–8). Luke mentions that Jesus ate fish after his resurrection (24:40–43)—hardly normal behavior for an apparition! These accounts can be dated to years, not centuries, after Jesus lived.

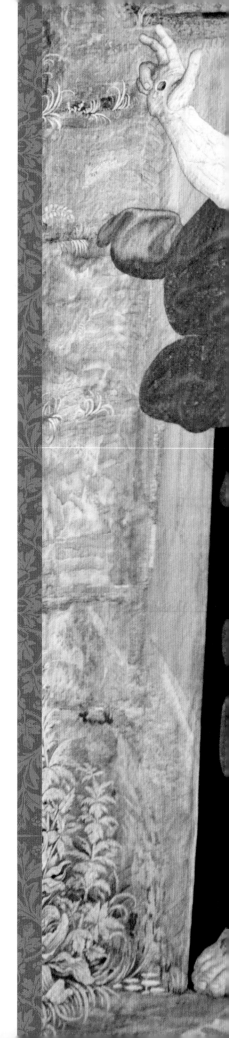

A message from
THE BIBLE
1 PETER 1:3

Praise God, the Father of our Lord Jesus Christ. God is so good, and by raising Jesus from death, he has given us new life and a hope that lives on.

WHAT'S THE POINT?
WHY THERE HAS TO BE A BODY

Why does it matter whether Jesus' resurrection is a physical reality or just a symbol? For Christians, the bodily resurrection is important for at least two reasons. First, as Paul argued, if God didn't raise Jesus from the dead, then there's little hope for any of us after death (see 1 Corinthians 15:16–18). Second, the fact that Jesus rose from the dead means that there's someone in heaven who can empathize with our struggles and intercede on our behalf. As the writer of Hebrews noted, *"We have a great high priest, who has gone into heaven, and he is Jesus the Son of God"* (Hebrews 4:14).

Tapestry detail from the Vatican Museums showing the resurrection of Jesus Christ. A scene based on the apocryphal Gospel of Peter

Women at the Empty Tomb
Fra Angelico (1395–1455)

101

POSTRESURRECTION APPEARANCES

Jesus' resurrection is recorded in numerous places in
the Bible and was reported by many eyewitnesses.
Paul records in 1 Corinthians 15:1–11 the longest list of
postresurrection appearances of Jesus.

MY FRIENDS, I WANT YOU TO REMEMBER THE MESSAGE I PREACHED
AND THAT YOU BELIEVED AND TRUSTED. YOU WILL BE SAVED BY THIS
MESSAGE, IF YOU HOLD FIRMLY TO IT. BUT IF YOU DON'T, YOUR FAITH
WAS ALL FOR NOTHING.

I TOLD YOU THE MOST IMPORTANT PART OF THE MESSAGE EXACTLY AS
IT WAS TOLD TO ME. THAT PART IS:

CHRIST DIED FOR OUR SINS,
AS THE SCRIPTURES SAY.
HE WAS BURIED,
AND THREE DAYS LATER
HE WAS RAISED TO LIFE,
AS THE SCRIPTURES SAY.
CHRIST APPEARED TO PETER, THEN TO THE TWELVE.
AFTER THIS, HE APPEARED
TO MORE THAN FIVE HUNDRED
OTHER FOLLOWERS.
MOST OF THEM ARE STILL ALIVE,
BUT SOME HAVE DIED.
HE ALSO APPEARED TO JAMES,
AND THEN TO ALL
OF THE APOSTLES.

FINALLY, HE APPEARED TO ME, EVEN THOUGH I AM LIKE SOMEONE
WHO WAS BORN AT THE WRONG TIME. I AM THE LEAST IMPORTANT
OF ALL THE APOSTLES. IN FACT, I CAUSED SO MUCH TROUBLE FOR GOD'S
CHURCH THAT I DON'T EVEN DESERVE TO BE CALLED AN APOSTLE. BUT
GOD TREATED ME WITH UNDESERVED GRACE! HE MADE ME WHAT I AM,
AND HIS GRACE WASN'T WASTED. I WORKED MUCH HARDER THAN ANY
OF THE OTHER APOSTLES, ALTHOUGH IT WAS REALLY GOD'S GRACE AT
WORK AND NOT ME. BUT IT DOESN'T MATTER IF I PREACHED OR IF THEY
PREACHED. ALL OF YOU BELIEVED THE MESSAGE JUST THE SAME.

BELOW ARE MANY OF THE OTHER NEW TESTAMENT STORIES OF JESUS' POSTRESURRECTION APPEARANCES:

MARY MAGDALENE SEES JESUS
Matthew 28:9–10; Mark 16:9; John 20:14–17

JESUS APPEARS TO HIS DISCIPLES
IN A LOCKED ROOM
John 20:19–29

JESUS WALKS WITH TWO FOLLOWERS TO EMMAUS
Luke 24:13–32

SEVEN DISCIPLES SEE JESUS ALONG
THE SHORE OF LAKE TIBERIAS
John 21:1–14

JESUS GIVES FINAL INSTRUCTIONS TO
HIS ELEVEN DISCIPLES
Matthew 28:16–20

JESUS APPEARS TO 500 PEOPLE AT ONCE
1 Corinthians 15:6

JAMES, JESUS' BROTHER, SEES JESUS
1 Corinthians 15:7

THE DISCIPLES SEE JESUS ASCEND TO HEAVEN
Luke 24:50–51; Acts 1:9–11

THE ASCENSION

Luke ends his Gospel account with a description of Jesus' ascent to heaven. This ascent is described in more detail in his next book (see Acts 1:1–11). The ascension represented an important turning point for Jesus and his followers.

After his resurrection, Jesus spent time (forty days to be exact, according to Acts 1:3) with his followers, instructing them how to carry on his work. He also made them promises, including the promise that the Holy Spirit would come upon them and give them power.

Jesus' ascension forever changed the relationship between God and humanity. The work he came to do had been completed, allowing each of us to connect with God in a new way. Before Christ's mission, we could only hope for a future reconciliation with God; now we can base our hope on the reality of Jesus' sacrifice. While the Spirit of God has existed since before time, the work of Jesus inaugurated a new kind of relationship in which God's Spirit lives inside his reconciled people, teaching and leading them in the ways of the kingdom.

But the ascension held another message too. In the Bible, ascent often symbolizes victory. Centuries before Christ, for example, the psalmist imagined God ascending a high mountain as he triumphed over his enemies (Psalm 68:18). In the eyes of his followers, Jesus' ascent to heaven put the exclamation mark on his victory over death and sin.

WHERE IS JESUS NOW?

According to the apostle Paul, Jesus was *"taken up to glory"* after preaching his message of hope to the nations (1 Timothy 3:16). But his work is far from finished. In Ephesians, Paul gave readers a glimpse behind the curtain of heaven, revealing the true significance of Jesus' ascension to glory. Paul declared that Jesus sits at God's right hand, ruling all things and working on behalf of his followers:

There Christ rules over all forces, authorities, powers, and rulers. He rules over all beings in this world and will rule in the future world as well. God has put all things under the power of Christ, and for the good of the church he has made him the head of everything. (Ephesians 1:21–22)

Saint Isaac's Cathedral
Interior of the main dome

THE COMING OF
THE HOLY SPIRIT

Before returning to heaven, Jesus promised to send his followers the Holy Spirit to guide and comfort them.

The Spirit will come and show the people of this world the truth about sin and God's justice and the judgment . . . . I have much more to say to you, but right now it would be more than you could understand. The Spirit shows what is true and will come and guide you into the full truth. The Spirit doesn't speak on his own. He will tell you only what he has heard from me, and he will let you know what is going to happen. The Spirit will bring glory to me by taking my message and telling it to you. (John 16:8–14)

The Greek word for spirit is "wind," or "breath," possibly indicating the mysterious nature of this promised comforter. Perhaps the true significance of the Spirit's coming is that it means the connection to God isn't severed by Jesus' departure. According to Paul, the Holy Spirit is God's reminder to his people that they *"belong only to him"* (2 Corinthians 1:22).

Pentecost, 1732
Jean Restout II (1692–1768)
Oil on canvas.
Louvre, Paris

A message from
THE BIBLE
EXODUS 23:20–23

I am sending an angel to protect you and to lead you into the land I have ready for you. Carefully obey everything the angel says, because I am giving him complete authority, and he won't tolerate rebellion. If you faithfully obey him, I will be a fierce enemy of your enemies. My angel will lead you into the land of the Amorites, Hittites, Perizzites, Canaanites, Hivites, and Jebusites, and I will wipe them out.

UNSEEN CHARACTERS
in the story

Depictions of angels are abundant in contemporary culture, where they inspire much curiosity and wonder. The merchandising of angels is everywhere—garden statues, greeting cards, costumes, tattoos, and more. Angels have been familiar characters on the screen as well—from the heartwarming Monica on *Touched by an Angel* to the scruffy Earl on *Saving Grace*. And who could forget the guileless Clarence from *It's a Wonderful Life*? Thanks in part to greeting cards and Hollywood, the very definition of angelic has come to mean "adorable," "cute." The real significance of these mysterious beings is often obscured by their popular depictions.

The angels of Scripture are creatures of fierce power and strong presence. People often trembled and sometimes ran when they saw angels—even people who were accustomed to interacting with God. Many times, the first thing an angel had to say to a human was something like, "Don't be afraid. Get up!" Other times, angels appeared more or less as guests or travelers, such as in the story of Abraham at Mamre (Genesis 18:1–15).

In the Bible, angels serve primarily as God's messengers. They were not dispatched to impart trivial news or perform menial tasks; often they revealed God's plan—and the deeper meaning behind it—to human participants in the drama. To encounter an angel meant that God was about to communicate critical information, deliver someone from a powerful threat, or perhaps pass divine judgment on someone.

In the stories that follow, angels bring hope to a forlorn mother, wrestle in the dirt with a self-involved patriarch, hover in midair with full intent to destroy Jerusalem, and aid in a daring prison escape. Angels provided the birth announcements for Isaac, Samson, and John the Baptist—revealing God's hidden purpose for these remarkable individuals. And the birth announcement about Jesus brought the good news that God's promised Messiah would soon be born. In each and every instance, angels were forceful representatives of God.

In fact, many of these stories make it difficult to differentiate between God's messenger and God. The angel may have been doing the talking, but the recipient of the message interpreted the words as coming from God. To encounter an angel was to experience the alarming and awe-inspiring fear of God.

A message from
THE BIBLE
GENESIS 16:4–16

Later, when Hagar knew she was going to have a baby, she became proud and treated Sarai hatefully. Then Sarai said to Abram, "It's all your fault! I gave you my slave woman, but she has been hateful to me ever since she found out she was pregnant. You have done me wrong, and you will have to answer to the LORD for this." Abram said, "All right! She's your slave—do whatever you want with her." Then Sarai began treating Hagar so harshly that she finally ran away.

Hagar stopped to rest at a spring in the desert on the road to Shur. While she was there, the angel of the LORD came to her and asked, "Hagar, where have you come from, and where are you going?"

She answered, "I'm running away from Sarai, my owner."

The angel said, "Go back to Sarai and be her slave. I will give you a son, who will be called Ishmael, because I have heard your cry for help. And someday I will give you so many descendants that no one will be able to count them all. But your son will live far from his relatives; he will be like a wild donkey, fighting everyone, and everyone fighting him." Hagar thought, "Have I really seen God and lived to tell about it?" So from then on she called him, "The God Who Sees Me." That's why people call the well between Kadesh and Bered, "The Well of the Living One Who Sees Me." Abram was 86 years old when Hagar gave birth to their son, and he named him Ishmael.

Hagar and Ishmael
Jean-Charles Cazin (1841–1901)

HAGAR
and the Angel of Provision

Hagar and Ishmael in the Wilderness, Karel Dujardin

Being female and unmarried provided little status or opportunity for success in the ancient world, so Hagar might seem an unlikely candidate for an angelic visitation. She was a slave belonging to Sarah (Sarai), Abraham's wife. God had promised Abraham a child; but since Sarah remained barren, Hagar was called on to serve as a surrogate and became pregnant by Abraham. Her pregnancy created enmity between the two women; and when Sarah began to mistreat her slave, Hagar ran away. Alone in the desert, Hagar was confronted by an angel who sent her back home, which she considered to be no less than an encounter with God himself (Genesis 16).

Fourteen years later, Sarah had a child of her own with Abraham, at which time she sent Hagar and her teenage son, Ishmael, away. Hagar expected her boy would die in the wilderness, but again an angel appeared. The angel comforted Hagar, assuring her that God had heard the cries of her son (Genesis 21:9–21).

WHAT'S THE POINT?
BOUNDARY-CROSSING COMPASSION

Some scholars see Hagar's story as a reminder that God's compassion is not limited to just one group of people. According to Genesis 21, God planned to make his covenant with Abraham's son Isaac, not Ishmael. Yet the angel promised a blessing for Hagar and Ishmael, too. Not only would they survive, God would make Ishmael into a great nation.

A message from
THE BIBLE

GENESIS 21:14–19

Early the next morning Abraham gave Hagar an animal skin full of water and some bread. Then he put the boy on her shoulder and sent them away. They wandered around in the desert near Beersheba, and after they had run out of water, Hagar put her son under a bush. Then she sat down a long way off, because she could not bear to watch him die. And she cried bitterly.

When God heard the boy crying, the angel of God called out to Hagar from heaven and said, "Hagar, why are you worried? Don't be afraid. I have heard your son crying. Help him up and hold his hand, because I will make him the father of a great nation." Then God let her see a well. So she went to the well and filled the skin with water, then gave some to her son.

Jacob Wrestling with the Angel
Alexandre-Louis Leloir (1843–1884)

A message from
THE BIBLE
GENESIS 32:24B–30

A man came and fought with Jacob until just before daybreak. When the man saw that he could not win, he struck Jacob on the hip and threw it out of joint. They kept on wrestling until the man said, "Let go of me! It's almost daylight."

"You can't go until you bless me," Jacob replied.

Then the man asked, "What is your name?"

"Jacob," he answered.

The man said, "From now on, your name will no longer be Jacob. You will be called Israel, because you have wrestled with God and with men, and you have won." Jacob said, "Now tell me your name."

"Don't you know who I am?" he asked. And he blessed Jacob.

Jacob said, "I have seen God face to face, and I am still alive." So he named the place Peniel.

JACOB
and an Angel of Redirection and Renewal

Jacob was Abraham's grandson. His children were the progenitors of the twelve tribes of Israel. But throughout most of Jacob's early life, he was a trickster or con man. His manipulative acquisition of his brother's birthright and blessing met with murderous threats from Esau. Ultimately, Jacob had to leave home for his own protection (Genesis 27:41–45). While away, he matched wits with his uncle Laban (his mother's brother) for a couple of decades before returning home. During this period of transition—first leaving home, then returning—he had two encounters with angels.

The first was a dream in which angels ascended and descended a "ladder," or "staircase," that reached all the way to heaven. Some think the vision served to show Jacob the close proximity of God, which would explain Jacob's startled response upon waking: *"The Lord is in this place, and I didn't even know it"* (Genesis 28:16).

Twenty years later, on his way home to meet Esau, an emboldened Jacob took part in an all-night wrestling match with an unidentified "man" (Genesis 32:24). Though this figure is not clearly identified in Genesis, the prophet Hosea later referred to him as an angel (Hosea 12:3–4). Jacob, however, considered the experience a *"face to face"* encounter with God. (His name for the location, Peniel, means "face of God." See Genesis 32:30.) Even after realizing that he was no match for his opponent, Jacob persevered, refusing to release the mysterious figure until he received a blessing. But Jacob also received a lifelong limp when his sparring partner struck his hip. Perhaps the significance of the injury was to remind Jacob of his dependence on God. After all, Jacob could no longer rely on his own strength to survive his reunion with his brother.

GIDEON
and an Angel of Counsel and Courage

During an era when judges ruled over Israel, the people experienced a recurring cycle of upheaval. First they would turn from God. As a result, they would become subject to a nearby enemy, which would lead them to cry out to God for help. Eventually, a national champion—or judge—would rise up and, with God's power, rescue the people from their enemies.

Some judges were natural leaders, but not Gideon. When we first meet Gideon, he is trying to thresh some grain in secret, hoping to avoid confrontation with the very enemies that God wanted him to fight. This unlikely hero would go on to defeat the numerous and powerful Midianites, using an army of only three hundred men (Judges 7). But it all began with a perplexing visit by an angel and a decision to believe (however reluctantly) in God's ability to come through for his people. Everything about the story reinforced the utterly lopsided nature of the conflict— Gideon's assessment of his family as the weakest in his tribe, his own reluctance to believe the angel, and the laughably small army he leads into battle. Gideon's story served as a reminder to generations of Israelites that the battle—and the much-hoped-for victory—belonged to God.

A message from THE BIBLE

JUDGES 6:11-14

One day an angel from the LORD went to the town of Ophrah and sat down under the big tree that belonged to Joash, a member of the Abiezer clan. Joash's son Gideon was nearby, threshing grain in a shallow pit, where he could not be seen by the Midianites.

The angel appeared and spoke to Gideon, "The LORD is helping you, and you are a strong warrior."

Gideon answered, "Please don't take this wrong, but if the LORD is helping us, then why have all of these awful things happened? We've heard how the LORD performed miracles and rescued our ancestors from Egypt. But those things happened long ago. Now the LORD has abandoned us to the Midianites."

Then the LORD himself said, "Gideon, you will be strong, because I am giving you the power to rescue Israel from the Midianites."

Gideon and the Fleece
French School (15th century)

DAVID
and the Angel of Destruction

Many people know about David's triumph over Goliath, his rise and reign as Israel's most famous king, and his shocking affair with Bathsheba and arranging for her husband to be killed in battle in an attempt to cover his indiscretion. Perhaps less known is David's experience with one of the most terrifying angels in the Bible.

Late in his career, David conducted a census of his troops—an act that met with God's disapproval. David's motives for the census were military in nature: he wanted to know how many people could serve in his army. In other words, he was showing signs of trusting in his own power rather than God's.

As was the case with Gideon's and Jacob's angelic encounters, this one served as a reminder that true strength comes from God. However, David's encounter produced far more terrifying results than the others.

After being allowed to choose his punishment, David saw an angel of destruction—who was witnessed by others as well—poised in midair, ready to destroy Jerusalem, the capital city of Israel. Seventy thousand people had already died across Israel. In his mercy, however, God withheld the angel's hand, and Jerusalem was spared (see 1 Chronicles 21).

A message from
THE BIBLE
1 CHRONICLES 21:7–30

David's order to count the people made God angry, and he punished Israel. David prayed, "I am your servant. But what I did was stupid and terribly wrong. Please forgive me."

The Lord said to Gad, one of David's prophets, "Tell David that I will punish him in one of three ways. But he will have to choose which one it will be."

Gad went to David and told him: "You must choose how the Lord will punish you: Will there be three years when the land won't grow enough food for its people? Or will your enemies constantly defeat you for three months? Or will the Lord send a horrible disease to strike your land for three days? Think about it and decide, because I have to give your answer to God who sent me."

David was miserable and said, "It's a terrible choice to make! But the Lord is kind, and I'd rather be punished by him than by anyone else."

So the Lord sent a horrible disease on Israel, and 70,000 Israelites died. Then he sent an angel to destroy the city of Jerusalem. But just as the angel was about to do that, the Lord felt sorry for all the suffering he had caused the people, and he told the angel, "Stop! They have suffered enough." This happened at the threshing place that belonged to Araunah the Jebusite.

David saw the Lord's angel in the air, holding a sword over Jerusalem. He and the leaders of Israel, who were all wearing sackcloth, bowed with their faces to the ground, and David prayed, "It's my fault! I sinned by ordering the people to be counted. They have done nothing wrong—they are innocent sheep. Lord God, please punish me and my family. Don't let the disease wipe out your people."

The Lord's angel told the prophet Gad to tell David that he must go to Araunah's threshing place and build an altar in honor of the Lord. David followed the Lord's instructions.

Araunah and his four sons were threshing wheat at the time, and when they saw the angel, the four sons ran to hide. Just then, David arrived, and when Araunah saw him, he stopped his work and bowed down....So David paid Araunah 600 gold coins for his threshing place. David built an altar and offered sacrifices to please the Lord and sacrifices to ask his blessing. David prayed, and the Lord answered him by sending fire down on the altar. Then the Lord commanded the angel to put the sword away. When David saw that the Lord had answered his prayer, he offered more sacrifices there at the threshing place, because he was afraid of the angel's sword and did not want to go all the way to Gibeon. That's where the sacred tent that Moses had made in the desert was kept, as well as the altar where sacrifices were offered to the Lord.

David, at the time of his defeat of Goliath, Donatello (c. 1386–1466)

DANIEL
and the Angels of Prophecy and Protection

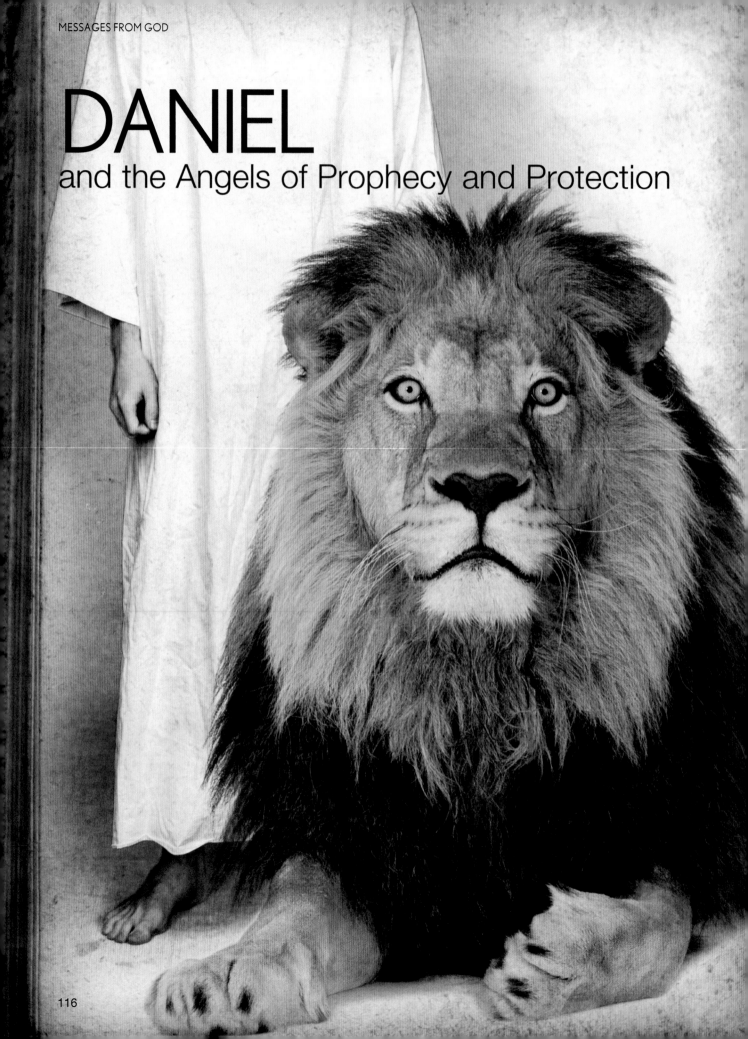

Daniel, the young man who was carried to Babylon with a number of captive Israelites, is well known for angelic encounters. His friends Shadrach, Meshach, and Abednego were miraculously spared from a fiery furnace, and Daniel himself survived a night in a den of hungry lions. Both events refer to an angel who was sent to protect God's faithful servants (Daniel 3:28; 6:22).

The book of Daniel also mentions other encounters, which provide further insight into the purpose of angels, as depicted in the Bible. First, angels provide protection. Michael the archangel is identified as *"the guardian angel of Israel"* (10:21) and the *"protector of [Daniel's] people"* (12:1). The Bible leaves much to the imagination when it comes to guardian angels and the battles they fight, but Daniel 10 mentions a conflict so intense that Michael himself had to intervene (10:12–14).

Angels also reveal God's plan for the future. The angel who visited Daniel came to show him what would happen to the Israelites. What follows is an apocalyptic vision of empires toppling each other as the end draws near (11:2–45). But there is a deeper meaning to the angel's cryptic prophecy: God is in control of all things. He will not let Daniel's people suffer indefinitely at the hands of others.

The angel describes events happening *"at the time God has decided"* (Daniel 11:29). He assures Daniel that God will protect his people through it all, even bringing back to life those who have already died (12:1–3). The angel's message bears a striking resemblance to another apocalyptic book: Revelation, which promises God's final victory over the forces of evil. Spiritual warfare is described in Revelation 12, and the enemies of God are thrown out of heaven by the archangel Michael and his army of angels.

According to the angel who spoke to Daniel, the deeper meaning of his message would remain *"secret until the end of time"* (Daniel 12:4). Yet for Daniel, the implications were clear: God will not abandon his people.

Daniel's Answer to the King, Briton Rivière

A message from THE BIBLE
DANIEL 10:2–19

Daniel wrote: For three weeks I was in sorrow. I ate no fancy food or meat, I drank no wine, and I put no olive oil on my face or hair. Then, on the twenty-fourth day of the first month, I was standing on the banks of the great Tigris River, when I looked up and saw someone dressed in linen and wearing a solid gold belt. His body was like a precious stone, his face like lightning, his eyes like flaming fires, his arms and legs like polished bronze, and his voice like the roar of a crowd. . . . I stood trembling, while the angel said:

"Daniel, don't be afraid! God has listened to your prayers since the first day you humbly asked for understanding, and he has sent me here. But the guardian angel of Persia opposed me for 21 days. Then Michael, who is one of the strongest guardian angels, came to rescue me from the kings of Persia. Now I have come here to give you another vision about what will happen to your people in the future."

While this angel was speaking to me, I stared at the ground, speechless. Then he appeared in human form and touched my lips. I said, "Sir, this vision has brought me great pain and has drained my strength. I am merely your servant. How can I possibly speak with someone so powerful, when I am almost too weak to get my breath?"

The angel touched me a second time and said, "Don't be frightened! God thinks highly of you, and he intends this for your good, so be brave and strong."

At this, I regained my strength and replied, "Please speak! You have already made me feel much better."

ZECHARIAH
and an Angel of Unexpected Bounty and Blessing

Angels appear at key points in the biblical accounts of the life and times of Jesus. Prior to his birth, God sent an angel to inform a priest named Zechariah that he and his wife Elizabeth would have a son (John the Baptist), who would prepare his people for the arrival of their Messiah.

Zechariah's skeptical reaction is easy to understand. He and his wife, devout followers of God, were elderly and childless. Still, because of his initial doubt, the angel rendered Zechariah unable to speak until the birth of the promised child. After John was born, the first words out of Zechariah's mouth were spoken in praise to God (Luke 1:62–64, 67–79).

WHAT'S THE POINT? **PROMISE KEPT**

Centuries before Zechariah, the prophet Malachi predicted God would send a *"messenger to prepare the way"* for the Lord—that is, for a Messiah who would rescue God's people (Malachi 3:1). By some accounts, God hadn't spoken to his people since Malachi's prophecy, which might also help to explain Zechariah's startled reaction to his angelic visitor. The angel's appearance had a deeper significance than just the promised birth of Zechariah's son; it demonstrated that God's plan to rescue his people was still very much on track.

A message from THE BIBLE
LUKE 1:8–20

One day Zechariah's group of priests were on duty, and he was serving God as a priest. According to the custom of the priests, he had been chosen to go into the Lord's temple that day and to burn incense, while the people stood outside praying. All at once an angel from the Lord appeared to Zechariah at the right side of the altar. Zechariah was confused and afraid when he saw the angel. But the angel told him:

"Don't be afraid, Zechariah! God has heard your prayers. Your wife Elizabeth will have a son, and you must name him John. His birth will make you very happy, and many people will be glad. Your son will be a great servant of the Lord. He must never drink wine or beer, and the power of the Holy Spirit will be with him from the time he is born.

John will lead many people in Israel to turn back to the Lord their God. He will go ahead of the Lord with the same power and spirit that Elijah had. And because of John, parents will be more thoughtful of their children. And people who now disobey God will begin to think as they ought to. This is how John will get people ready for the Lord."

Zechariah said to the angel, "How will I know this is going to happen? My wife and I are both very old."

The angel answered, "I am Gabriel, God's servant, and I was sent to tell you this good news. You have not believed what I have said. So you will not be able to say a thing until all this happens. But everything will take place when it is supposed to."

An Angel Tells Zechariah That He Will Have a Son
14th century mosaic
Baptistery, Venice, Italy

Angels Among Us

Most major religions acknowledge angelic beings, and many see angels as ways to connect with the divine. But even outside of religious circles, angels continue to be a popular topic.

It might be true that this cultural fascination with angels hints at some desire for God. It may even speak to the hope that if we face the reality of God's existence, we hope we can encounter him in such a way that neither his presence nor his power will terrify us.

The Dream of Saint Joseph
Philippe de Champaigne (1602–1674)

MARY AND JOSEPH
and an Angel of Challenge and Change

God prepared to enter the world in human form as the child of a simple carpenter and a humble young girl. The angel Gabriel delivered the startling news to Mary first (Luke 1:26–38). She was understandably bewildered at how she could possibly give birth, since she was a virgin; yet she submitted to the will of God.

When Joseph learned of Mary's pregnancy, he knew it wasn't his child, and he decided to end their engagement quietly. To his credit, his chief desire was to spare Mary from being the object of local gossip and humiliation. But when an angel then appeared to Joseph in a dream to assure him that Mary had done nothing improper, Joseph decided to take Mary as his wife after all (Matthew 1:18–25). As a result, the two of them proved instrumental in fulfilling a centuries-old promise of God's redemption.

Later, Mary and Joseph protected the infant Jesus from the wrath of King Herod, fleeing their home for the safety of Egypt. Angels directed the couple, telling them when to leave and when to return (Matthew 2:16–23).

WHAT'S THE POINT?
FAR YET NEAR

Angels must have been an intimidating sight, considering how often they had to tell people not to be afraid (as was the case with Mary). As such, angels served as a reminder of God's transcendence—his "otherness." Yet these angels also closed the gap between humans and God, reminding those they visited that God was intimately involved in their lives—that he was as close as an angelic messenger.

A message from
THE BIBLE
MATTHEW 1:18–25

This is how Jesus Christ was born. A young woman named Mary was engaged to Joseph from King David's family. But before they were married, she learned that she was going to have a baby by God's Holy Spirit. Joseph was a good man and did not want to embarrass Mary in front of everyone. So he decided to quietly call off the wedding. While Joseph was thinking about this, an angel from the Lord appeared to him in a dream. The angel said, "Joseph, the baby that Mary will have is from the Holy Spirit. Go ahead and marry her. Then after her baby is born, name him Jesus, because he will save his people from their sins." So the Lord's promise came true, just as the prophet had said, "A virgin will have a baby boy, and he will be called Immanuel," which means "God is with us."

After Joseph woke up, he and Mary were soon married, just as the Lord's angel had told him to do. But they did not sleep together before her baby was born. Then Joseph named him Jesus.

PETER
and an Angel of Release and Rescue

After Jesus' death, resurrection, and return to heaven, the Holy Spirit arrived to comfort and empower his followers (Acts 2). During Jesus' trial and execution, even those closest to him had been guilty of betraying, denying, and deserting him. Yet now, with the Holy Spirit to help, they began to speak and act with boldness. Very soon, their audacity met with resistance, and Peter found himself imprisoned. Even so, he was sleeping soundly when he had an angelic encounter in the depths of his jail. (The angel had to physically poke him to wake him up! See Acts 12:7.)

In this instance, only Peter was aware of the angel's presence. In fact, he thought he was dreaming at first. It was only after he found himself on the street, alone and free, that he realized the experience was indeed genuine. He wasn't the only one surprised, either; when he arrived at a home filled with friends who were praying for his release, it took some time for them to believe it was really Peter (Acts 12:12–16).

The angel in this case may have been God's tool for ensuring the survival of the early church. Peter was a key figure in the church, and the account of his miraculous rescue from prison may have emboldened Christians facing persecution to stand firm.

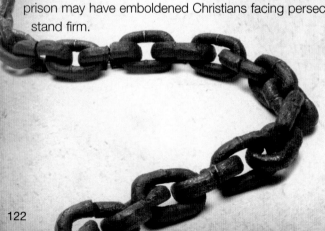

A message from
THE BIBLE
ACTS 12:1–16

At that time King Herod caused terrible suffering for some members of the church. He ordered soldiers to cut off the head of James, the brother of John. When Herod saw that this pleased the Jewish people, he had Peter arrested during the Festival of Thin Bread. He put Peter in jail and ordered four squads of soldiers to guard him. Herod planned to put him on trial in public after the festival. While Peter was being kept in jail, the church never stopped praying to God for him.

The night before Peter was to be put on trial, he was asleep and bound by two chains. A soldier was guarding him on each side, and two other soldiers were guarding the entrance to the jail. Suddenly an angel from the Lord appeared, and light flashed around in the cell. The angel poked Peter in the side and woke him up. Then he said, "Quick! Get up!"

The chains fell off his hands, and the angel said, "Get dressed and put on your sandals."

Peter did what he was told. Then the angel said, "Now put on your coat and follow me."

Peter left with the angel, but he thought everything was only a dream. They went past the two groups of soldiers, and when they came to the iron gate to the city, it opened by itself. They went out and were going along the street, when all at once the angel disappeared.

Peter now realized what had happened, and he said, "I am certain that the Lord sent his angel to rescue me from Herod and from everything the Jewish leaders planned to do to me." Then Peter went to the house of Mary the mother of John whose other name was Mark. Many of the Lord's followers had come together there and were praying.

Peter knocked on the gate, and a servant named Rhoda came to answer. When she heard Peter's voice, she was too excited to open the gate. She ran back into the house and said Peter was standing there.

"You are crazy!" everyone told her. But she kept saying it was Peter. Then they said, "It must be his angel." But Peter kept on knocking, until finally they opened the gate. They saw him and were completely amazed.

The Liberation of St. Peter
Alessandro Turchi (1579–1649)

123

ACKNOWLEDGMENTS
CREDITS

EDITORIAL SOURCES

BOOKS

- *Bible Atlas and Companion*, Christopher D. Hudson. Barbour. 2007
- *Christian Theology*, Millard Erickson, Baker Academic. 1998.
- *Holman Bible Dictionary*, Trent C. Butler (ed), Broadman & Holman Publishers, 1991
- *International Standard Bible Encyclopedia*, Electronic Edition Parsons Technology, Inc.1998
- *Miracles*, C.S. Lewis. HarperOne, 2001.
- *Miracles or Magic?* Andre Kole, Harvest House Publishers, 1987
- *The Archaeological Study Bible*, Zondervan, 2005
- *The New International Dictionary of the Bible*, J.D. Douglas & Merrill C. Tenney (ed); Zondervan, 1987
- *The QuickNotes Commentary Series*, Christopher D. Hudson. Barbour. 2011
- *The Truth Behind the Da Vinci Code*, Richard Abanes, Harvest House Publishers, 2004
- *Truth and Fiction in the Da Vinci Code*, Bart D. Ehrman, Oxford University Press, 2004
- *Tyndale Bible Dictionary*, Walter Elwell, Ph.D., Philip W. Comfort, Ph.D. (ed), Tyndale, 2001

ART SOURCES

Art Resource

Persian and Medean Warriors.
Relief from the Audience Hall of Darius I (Apadana), eastern stairway. Achaemenid dynasty, 6th–5th c. BCE.
Location: Persepolis, Iran
Bridgeman-Giraudon / Art Resource, NY
ART88602

The Cave of Ein-Gedi, the spring of the kid which waters the region that drops down to the Red Sea. Here David hid from King Saul.
Location: Oasis, En-Gedi, Israel
Erich Lessing / Art Resource, NY
ART68690

Birds Entering the Ark. Mosaic.
Location: S. Marco, Venice, Italy
Scala / Art Resource, NY
ART46630

The Hills Between Beit Shemesh and Jerusalem,
where Samson Fought Against the Philistines.
Location: Beth-Shemesh, Israel
Erich Lessing / Art Resource, NY
ART44586

The Destruction of Sodom by Fire, detail.
Location: Musee des Beaux-Arts, Orleans, France
Scala/White Images / Art Resource, NY
ART429046

The Dream of Saint Joseph, 1642–3.
Champaigne, Philippe de (1602–1674)
Oil on canvas
Location: National Gallery, London, Great Britain
National Gallery, London / Art Resource, NY
Image Reference: ART373638

The Tomb of Lazarus at Jerusalem, ca. 1900
Anonymous, 19th century
Photo Verdeau/ Adoc-photos/Art Resource, NY.
Location: Tomb of Lazarus, Bethany, Israel
Adoc-photos / Art Resource, NY
Image Reference: ART327674

Roman Jugs from Cana, Israel. Terracotta.
Location: Studium Biblicum Franciscanum, Jerusalem, Israel
Erich Lessing / Art Resource, NY
Image Reference: ART204288

Jesus Healing the Hemophiliac Woman.
Early Christian mosaic.
Location: S. Apollinare Nuovo, Ravenna, Italy
Erich Lessing / Art Resource, NY
Image Reference: ART20260

The Horns of Jericho were used during Joshua's conquest
The Oasis of Jericho seen against the surrounding desert.
Location: Jericho, Israel
Erich Lessing / Art Resource, NY
ART19526

Christ Before Pilate.
Beck, Walter (1864–1954)
Location: Smithsonian American Art Museum, Washington, DC, U.
Smithsonian American Art Museum, Washington, DC / Art Resource, NY
ART182992

Pentecost.
Restout, Jean (1663–1702)
Location: Louvre, (Museum), Paris, France
Photo Credit: © RMN-Grand Palais / Art Resource, NY
ART169356

The Three Angels Appearing to Abraham
Tiepolo, Giambattista (1696–1770)
Location: Accademia, Venice, Italy'
Cameraphoto Arte, Venice / Art Resource, NY
ART166892

The Infant Samuel Being Offered to the High Priest Eli.
Gothic manuscript. 15th CE.
Location: Bibliotheque Nationale, Paris, France
Erich Lessing / Art Resource, NY
ART15681

An Angel Tells Saint Zachary That He Will Have a son.
14th century mosaic
Location: Baptistery, S. Marco, Venice, Italy
Erich Lessing / Art Resource, NY
ART131460

Mother Teresa (1910–1997).
Roman Catholic nun, founder of the Missionaries of Charity.
Photo Credit: Album / Art Resource, NY
ALB1468436

Bridgeman

Solomon Before the Ark of the Covenant, 1747
Le Sueur, Blaise Nicolas (1716–83)
Musee des Beaux-Arts, Caen, France
Giraudon
XIR 173494

Christ crowned with thorns (wood)
Filipino School (20th Century)
Private Collection
Photo © Boltin Picture Library

GoodSalt

Babylon
Pacific Press
Image ID: pppas0100

Moses
Erik Stenbakken
Image ID: ebsps0262

Dover Electronic Clip Art
Bible Illustrations
120 Great Paintings of the Life of Jesus

FotoSearch
www.fotosearch.com
Christian Faith Vol. 1, Christian Faith Vol. 2, Christian Faith Vol. 3

Dreamstime
www.dreamstime.com

All other images:
iStock Photo, www.istockphoto.com
ThinkStock, www.thinkstock.com

HISTORY AND MISSION OF AMERICAN BIBLE SOCIETY

AMERICAN BIBLE SOCIETY

Established in 1816, American Bible Society's history is closely intertwined with the history of a nation whose founding preceded its own by less than a generation. In fact, the Society's early leadership reads like a Who's Who of patriots and other notable Americans of the time. Its first president was Elias Boudinot, formerly the President of the Continental Congress. John Jay, John Quincy Adams, DeWitt Clinton, and chronicler of the new nation James Fennimore Cooper also played significant roles, as would Rutherford B. Hayes and Benjamin Harrison in later generations.

From the beginning, the Bible Society's mission was to respond to the civic and spiritual needs of a fast-growing, diverse population in a rapidly expanding nation. From the new frontier beyond the Appalachian Mountains, missionaries sent back dire reports of towns that did not have a single copy of the Bible to share among its citizens. State and local Bible Societies did not have the resources, network, or capability of filling this growing need. Only a national organization would be able to do so. Once founded, ABS committed itself to organizational and technological innovation. No longer subject to British restrictions, ABS could set up its own printing plants, develop better qualities of paper and ink, and establish a network of colporteurs to get the Bibles to the people who needed them.

Reaching out to diverse audiences has always been at the heart of ABS's mission. Scriptures were made available to Native American peoples in their own languages—in Delaware in 1818, followed soon by Mohawk, Seneca, Ojibwa, Cherokee, and others. French and Spanish Bibles were published for the Louisiana Territory, Florida, and the Southwest. By the 1890s ABS was printing or distributing Scriptures in German, Portuguese, Chinese, Italian, Russian, Danish, Polish, Hungarian, Czech, and other languages to meet the spiritual needs of an increasing immigrant population. In 1836, seventy-five years before the first Braille Bibles were produced, ABS was providing Scriptures to the blind in "raised letter" editions. Responding to the need for Bibles in the languages and formats that speak most deeply to people's hearts continues to be a priority of ABS. Through its partnerships with other national Bible Societies, ABS can provide some portion of Scripture in almost any language that has a written form. It has also been able to provide Braille Scriptures for the blind; recorded Scriptures for the visually impaired, dyslexic, and people who have not yet learned to read; as well as Bible stories in sign language for the deaf.

The Bible Society's founders and their successors have always understood the Bible as a text that can speak to people's deepest needs during in times of crisis. ABS distributed its first Scriptures to the military in 1817 when it provided New Testaments to the crew of the USS *John Adams,* a frigate that had served in the War of 1812 and was continuing its service to the country by protecting the American Coast from pirates. During the Civil War, ABS provided Testaments to both northern and southern forces, and has continued to provide Bibles and Testaments to the U.S. military forces during every subsequent war, conflict, and operation. During the painful post-Reconstruction era when Jim Crow laws prevailed in many parts of the nation, ABS was able to provide Scriptures to African Americans through its partnership with the Agency Among Colored People of the South and through the historic Black churches. This faith that the Word of God speaks in special ways during times of crisis continues to inform ABS's mission. In recent years the Bible Society has produced Scripture booklets addressing the needs of people with HIV and AIDS and for those experiencing profound loss due to acts of terrorism and natural disasters.

Translation and scholarship are key components to the Bible Society's mission of faithfully and powerfully communicating the Word of God. In the mid-twentieth century, ABS, in partnership with the United Bible Societies, developed innovative theories and practices of translation, under the leadership of Eugene A. Nida. First, they insisted that all of the Bible translations they sponsored be done exclusively by native speakers, with biblical and linguistic experts serving only as translation consultants to provide technical support and guidance. From the lively and heart-felt translations that resulted, Bible Society scholars were able to see the power of translations that were rendered not on a word-for-word basis, but on a meaning-for-meaning basis that respected the natural rhythms and idioms of the target languages. This practice of "functional

equivalence" translation led to a new line of Bible translations in English and was, in part, responsible for the explosion of new translations of the Bible that came out in the past thirty years. These include the Bible Society's own *Good News Translation* and *Contemporary English Version*, as well as other non-English translations.

As an organization dedicated to preparing well-researched, faithful translations, ABS has necessarily committed itself to the pursuit of scholarly excellence. In cooperation with the United Bible Societies, ABS has helped develop and publish authoritative Greek and Hebrew texts, Handbooks on the different books of the Bible, dictionaries, and other technical aids. To provide the most up-to-date training and the broadest access to all the relevant disciplines, the Nida Institute for Biblical Scholarship offers professional development seminars and workshops, hosts symposia, and publishes a journal and monograph series, all in a effort to ensure that translators communicate the Word of God powerfully to God's people around the world. For churches and readers seeking a deeper understanding of the Bible and its background, ABS has developed study Bibles, multimedia video translations with DVD extras, Scriptures in special formats, and website resources.

For almost two centuries, ABS has maintained its commitment to innovation and excellence. While the challenges it has faced over the years have changed, the Society's mission has remained constant—*to make the Bible available to every person in a language and format each can understand and afford so all people may experience its life-changing message.*

To find out more about American Bible Society please go to www.americanbible.org or www.bibles.com.